History of India

A Captivating Guide to Ancient India, Medieval Indian History, and Modern India Including Stories of the Maurya Empire, the British Raj, Mahatma Gandhi, and More

Free Bonus from Captivating History (Available for a Limited time)

Hi History Lovers!

Now you have a chance to join our exclusive history list so you can get your first history ebook for free as well as discounts and a potential to get more history books for free! Simply visit the link below to join.

Captivatinghistory.com/ebook

Also, make sure to follow us on Facebook, Twitter and Youtube by searching for Captivating History.

Contents

Introduction

India is a land of mystery, richness, and deep spiritual discovery. Every facet of this ancient land seems scented with the famous spices that lured European traders to its shores more than five centuries ago. Here, Muslims, Hindus, Christians, Sikhs, and Buddhists live shoulder to shoulder in a crowded world of multiple gods and juxtaposed pilgrimage routes, each one perfectly peaceful in their own beliefs and traditions.

More than one billion people live on the Indian subcontinent, working in a range of industries that begins in the agricultural sector and ends in the high-tech business world of Delhi. Intensified manufacturing and digital technologies have brought modern India into the global market, trading in communications software, customer service, and IT management—but these are far from the technologies and industries that put this ancient land on every map. Long before the British Raj or the tea trade, India was beloved for its spices and jewels. For much of history, India provided the majority of the world's diamonds from its own mines. Some of those sparkling, perfect gems grace the likes of the British crown jewels.

Cinnamon, cardamom, turmeric, silks, and textiles remain at the forefront of the Indian market, while the country's cities embrace office work in the form of healthcare, insurance, and banking administration. Where now there are 21st-century business clothes and high-rises, once there were only religious robes and fish markets. In India, however, modernity need not take the place of antiquity; in the many cities and towns of the subcontinent, traditionally robed monks walk the streets chanting their spells alongside a parade in honor of the Hindu God Shiva, while a block away hundreds of English-speaking Indians set down their briefcases and log onto the internet to begin the day's work.

India is quite unique in the way it has brought its ancient histories and traditions with it into the modern age. Ganesh and Shiva have accompanied their people from the Indus River Valley–the spring of Indian civilization–down the Ganges and forward through time.

Chapter 1 – The Indus River Valley

It is easy to look at a modern political map and recognize the country that inhabits the immense subcontinent of southern Asia. Most of its borders are defined by warm oceans; the northeast delineated by the towering Himalayan mountains. Yet, at the northwestern edge of modern India, a crucial piece has been removed: that of the Indus River Valley, which lies in today's Pakistan. Despite the political separation, it was from this fertile section of the subcontinent that Indian civilization once sprang.

Just as the Euphrates and Tigris Rivers became the cradle of civilization to the ancient people of Mesopotamia (modern Iraq), the Indus River Valley and the Sarasvati River provided the resources and safety early south Asian people needed to build cities and consolidate their wealth. As early as 3000 BCE, the river valley flourished with tall buildings, agriculture, and trade that stretched from modern Afghanistan into northern India. As many as six million people may have lived here during the peak of the Indus-Sarasvati civilization, around 4,000 years ago.

The most important feature of the Indus Valley was—and still is— the river that stretches southwest across the entirety of Pakistan until meeting the Arabian Sea. It was an alluring stretch of fertile, water-adjacent land for nomads and immigrants even thousands of years before large cities appeared. The influx of ideas helped solidify the valley's future as a permanent settlement, while its inhabitants learned to cultivate sesame, rice, peas, dates, and sugarcane. They used cotton and hemp for textiles and created fire-baked clay bricks for buildings.

Thanks to a love of archaeological pursuit that became highly fashionable during the reign of England's Queen Victoria, multiple sites were discovered and cataloged along the Indus River by Indian and British treasure hunters. The first archaeological proof of the powerful and ancient Indian culture came from Harappa, thus causing the civilization and culture of these early people to often be referred to as Harappan. The ruins of the city, first rediscovered in 1826, are located in the Sahiwal District of Pakistan, near the border of India. Discovery of Harappa by those researchers challenged the belief of most Western historians and archaeologists that the only significant human settlements in that part of the world were Iraqi.

The city was subject to an intensive archaeological expedition in 1920 and 1921, a project led by Rai Bahadur Daya Ram Sahni and the Archaeological Survey of India. From Sahni and his successors' excavations, historians learned that the Indus Valley people of Harappa and other contemporary cities along the Indus and Sarasvati were exceptionally well-structured. They built homes, temples, and public buildings of brick and arranged these in neat, even rows and squares. The largest Harappa building was found at the site of the ancient city Mohenjo-daro, home of a public work called the Great Bath. This building—along with every structure in each of these cities—was connected via underground ducts to a city-wide drainage system that rivaled the modern systems used by the archaeologists themselves.

Harappans enjoyed all the natural resources necessary to produce surplus food and promote trade and permanent communal living. Since both river systems flooded reliably twice a year, residents were able to sow and reap two harvests per year and provide for their families as well as keep food stockpiled. These simple people lived in family groups and cultivated wheat, barley, cotton, and hemp while often keeping several cows, sheep, and goats. It was the Neolithic Revolution: a defining period of south Asian history during which people shifted from traditional nomadic hunting and gathering methods and into an agrarian lifestyle. For those early Indians, the center of the revolution was the floodplains. Possibly the world's oldest cities lay within those one million square kilometers (386,000 square miles), characterized not only by carefully built brick buildings but miniature sculptures, artwork, religious texts, and commercial artifacts like personal seals used to identify trade products. Clay seals and tablets feature untranslatable writing and inscribed drawings of elephants, lions, and rhinoceros.

The Sarasvati people developed regular trade routes, methods of sturdy shipbuilding, and navigation so that they might visit the lands to the east and west, including Mesopotamia and Egypt. There, they brought their own gold, copper, timber, ivory, and cotton, and purchased bronze, tin, silver, and soapstone to bring back to India. Archaeologists have found many of these items in unnatural locations, such as bronze, not native to the Indus Valley—proving the link between neighboring groups and cultures.

Hundreds of excavations at Harappa sites such as Rupar and Kalibangan did not reveal many examples of specialized artifacts that are normally an integral part of ancient culture: weaponry. There have been copper spears unearthed at these places, as well as collections of clay balls assumed to have been used in defense of the city, but these are few and artworks portraying any sort of warfare are very few and far between. Though it would be naïve to assume the early Indians of the Indus Valley were totally without violence and conflict, theirs does seem to have been a culture of peace. The farmers and city-builders of the Indus Valley civilization thrived from about 7000 to 3300 BCE.

Chapter 2 – Mythology of the Vedic Age

"One day at sunrise, after his morning ablutions in the waters of the Sarasvati, Srila Vyasadeva sat down to meditate. The great sage saw certain anomalies in the fiber of the millennium…He foresaw that the life of everything material would be cut short for lack of virtue."

(From the *Bhagavata Purana*)

The ancient Indians believed that before the dawn of creation, Lord Vishnu, the Preserver, slept in the Ocean of All Causes with a giant, many-hooded serpent as his bed. As he slept, a lotus sprouted from his navel in which was concealed Brahma, the god of Creation. During the day, Brahma creates our world and the creatures who live on it, and during the night, everything he made is absorbed back into him. When it is time for the world to be destroyed, Shiva will appear to wipe all of our world away.

This was the creation story of India's first major religious group whose beliefs would come to be recorded in the four Vedic texts. The Vedic religion, to which these and other archaeological artifacts relate, was an important part of ancient Indian culture as many as 6,000 years ago. Their texts were called the Rig-Veda, the Sama-Veda, the Yajur-Veda, and the Atharva-Veda. These works, originally passed from priest to priest by spoken word, weren't written down until about the 8th century BCE.

Throughout the four Vedas, a fantastic history of India is written, in which various pseudo-humanistic gods haphazardly create, destroy, and visit the earth to participate in a plethora of wars of justice. According to ancient beliefs, the Vedic gods were able to inhabit any of the three planes of existence: the universe, the earth, and the spaces in between. The central creation story as written in the Vedas includes far more detail after Brahma is born. One such tale is that of the god Indra, king of the utmost heavens, who became drunk on a special beverage called soma and then released all the rivers, rains, storms, and lightning of the world by slaying a dragon.

Modern India has a wealth of ancient artifacts from the Vedic people of that early era. Objects like clay pots, administrative seals, toys, and statues are highly prized in private collections and museums the world over. Though these items can tell us a great deal about early India, the language used on the seals has been lost to antiquity. Nobody knows how to decipher the strange lettering, but thankfully, like their neighbors the Egyptians, the Vedic people made liberal use of pictograms. A careful study of these pictograms and statues reveals something amazing: many of the religious symbols and ceremonies of the Vedic culture almost perfectly match those of today's Hindus.

Clues from the Sarasvati archaeological sites reveal a culture whose priests wore dots on their foreheads, whose married women painted the part in their hair red, and whose religious practitioners folded their legs together in what yogis call "lotus" position while praying. Images chiseled out of clay and stone thousands of years ago show a meditating man who bears a strong resemblance to the Hindu's Lord Shiva. The similarities are incredible, and they serve to strengthen the ties between modern and ancient India and denote an indigenous culture of all the lands in which the Sarasvati once lived.

The Vedic religion is believed to have begun shifting into a structure that more closely represents Hinduism by the 5th century BCE, though the Vedas remain the central focus of Hinduism today. The people who first read and spoke of them do not much resemble those who chant the Rig-Veda now; however, the former was a largely pastoral people whose livelihoods depended on raising animals for meat and milk.

Until about 1500 BCE, those who believed in the story of sleeping Lord Vishnu and the lotus universe lived in small urban communities that were linked to one another mostly via the waterways of the Land of Seven Rivers. Sarasvati homes and temples featured a fire pit, around which people would gather and worship Indra as a fire god. Priests and many Hindu followers continue this practice today, chanting thousands of hymns together that were passed down orally for millennia. The modern version of that Vedic fire god is Agni, who represents the sun, the hearth fire, lightning, and the flames of sacred sacrificial offerings.

The true difference between Hinduism and the Vedic religion of ancient India is complex, but one might say that the first urges its followers to search for truth, and the second urges them to honor the traditions of the past. That initial curiosity for meaning and truth is perhaps embodied best by the following Vedic poem, which questions even its own story of creation:

> Who really knows, and who can swear,
>
> How creation came, when or where!
>
> Even gods came after creation's day,
>
> Who really knows, who can truly say
>
> When and how did creation start?
>
> Did He do it? Or did He not?
>
> Only He, up there, knows, maybe;
>
> Or perhaps, not even He.

— Rig Veda 10.129.1-7

One billion members of the Hindu faith inhabit the world today, and although they are spread throughout 150 countries worldwide, most of them still live in India. The colorful stories of many-limbed gods with blue skin and a penchant for battle have survived much longer than any other human mythology to date. Thus, the Vedic values and lifestyle, which are interwoven into Hinduism, remain a pillar of Indian history, culture, and identity.

Chapter 3 – Aryan India and the Great Vedic Debate

The Indus Valley/Harappan culture went into decline after 1900 BCE, as did the Sarasvati River. Certainly, this was not a coincidence. Other factors that have been cited as fundamental in the decay and disappearance of the people who built Harappa and Mohenjo-daro, including massive earthquakes, floods, and the lack of warfare technology. Likely for all these reasons, the people who built their world around the Sarasvati and the Indus Rivers abandoned their cities, wrote no more upon clay tablets, and faded into the background of a landscape they had once dominated. As the culture died, a new one moved in with a group of northwestern Asians: the Aryans.

The Aryans, a nomadic people, did not overtake the cities of the Sarasvati but probably moved in peacefully over the Kush mountains with their cattle, looking for somewhere their animals could graze. The newcomers to the fertile floodplains liked the lands they found on the other side of the Himalayas, and they continued farther along the Indus and Sarasvati as had the Harappan people, intermingling with the local people in their few remaining communities over the next four millennia. It was a time of monumental importance to India, both as a landmass and in terms of its identity.

The Aryan people bonded with the Sarasvati to such an extent in many places that the two cultures became one, with beliefs and traditions merging together as people started to speak the Aryan language and the Aryans adopting the agricultural practices of the Sarasvati. Though there are no written records of what exactly took place during this phase of India's history, there is no physical evidence of a hostile takeover. It seems that the migration sparked friendly intermingling until a new culture emerged, and the cattle-herders settled in their own cities along the Indus and down along the drying riverbed of the Sarasvati.

Researchers believe that it was these Aryan people, and not the original Indus Valley inhabitants, who actually wrote the Vedic texts that would become Hinduism's most important literature. This summation was made based on archaeological and cultural clues from the Harappan sites. If the Aryans wrote the first Vedic and therefore Hindu myths, then it was not the indigenous Indians who developed this important belief system. Perhaps a viable theory is that of the mixed influence of both the Harrapans and the Aryans, who came together to create the Vedas just as peacefully as they came together to share the land.

Chapter 4 – Alexander the Great

In ancient Macedonia, 6,000 kilometers (4,000 miles) away from the Indian subcontinent, a ruler unlike any other came to power. History remembers him as Alexander the Great, the young emperor who spread Greek culture to half the world at the tip of his sword. In 326 BCE, the conqueror set his sights on the Indus River Valley after coming fresh off a successful campaign in Persia. It was a somewhat metaphorical challenge since Alexander wished to rule over the entire known world—maps of the ancient Greeks and Macedonians only went as far out as the Arabian Sea.

In the 4th century BCE, India was populated by the mixed people of both Dravidian and Aryan ancestry, whose political groups were numerous throughout the landscape. Though the people shared a basic culture, they were organized into a multitude of small kingdoms and city-states; there was no de facto leader of the land. For a would-be conqueror, this only made the job simpler as he could effectively march upon each successive polity and defeat one after the other without facing the backlash of an all-powerful ruler with armies the size of his own.

With 45,000 soldiers, Alexander faced his next colonial enemy at the east side of the Indus River. Prepared with the best ships, he planned to navigate down the Indus westward, crossing into the first urban settlement he found there, at Taxila. Alexander's troops easily won the quick surrender of Taxila without so much as a battle, whereupon several Macedonian commanders were left in charge of the town while the army marched southward. Being of Greek descent, the Macedonian army was exceptionally skilled at seafaring, but this particular conquest called for extensive overland ventures. There were 160 kilometers (100 miles) between the Indus and the Hydaspes Rivers; the emperor bade his troops to deconstruct their boats and carry the pieces to the next waterway. In this fashion, the journey between rivers took two months, including deconstruction and reconstruction time. On the other side of the Hydaspes awaited the kingdom of Porus.

King Porus was a famous and fierce ruler of the lands between the Hydaspes and Acesines Rivers, a region now called Punjab. He was over six feet tall, a marked aberration of height and size in that time and place, and a fearsome warrior on his feet or astride an elephant. Porus did not deign to allow the Macedonians to rule his kingdom without earning that right and so he mustered his own army to try to defeat them. It was a strange battle between men, elephants, and horses. The defending army was equipped with bows and arrows which were operated by holding the bow down with one foot while pulling the string back as far as possible. In addition to soldiers, Porus had 200 trained war elephants in the fight who took their job seriously.

The clash at Hydaspes was probably the most formidable endured by the Macedonian army during its time in India. It stretched on for days while Alexander maneuvered his horses and troops across the river. Though Porus' own forces were courageous and clever, they were ultimately beaten by Alexander's. The Macedonian emperor was impressed by his adversary, however, and proposed a compromise in lieu of an outright takeover of the king's lands.

Offered a role at the emperor's side as he continued to plow through India, Porus agreed and kept his kingdom as a subordinate leader under the Macedonian emperor. His knowledge and support were no doubt a great boon to the conquering army as it marched onward, this time to the east.

Just as the Dravidians and Aryans before him, Alexander the Great was fixated on the Indus River Valley. Even after thousands of years of human habitation, India's main waterway and floodplain were still the most valuable part of the land, providing not only a freshwater source but adjacent agricultural plots fertile and vast enough to feed cities full of citizens and soldiers. As such, the valley was not without its own local authority and protectorate, and after his monumental fight with King Porus, Alexander thought better of moving farther west along the path of the Indus. Instead, he shifted his plans and declared that the army would move along the Ganga, a waterway which had largely succeeded that of the old Sarasvati in location and importance.

The next adversary Alexander faced was Dhana Nanda, emperor of a vast tract of dynastic territory in the eastern section of modern India. Nanda was equipped with thousands of soldiers and more elephants even than King Porus, a fact that did nothing to dissuade the ambitious 30-year-old Alexander. It did, however, frighten his war-weary troops, most of whom had already been marching with the army for several years. By the time the Macedonian army reached the Beas River, just short of its intended destination, the invading troops had made an important decision: with or without Alexander the Great, they were throwing down their arms and returning home at long last. They were faced with the terrifying rumors of thousands of war elephants awaiting their arrival on the eastern side of the Ganga River. Though the Ganga is often referred to as the Ganges, the Hindi pronunciation is, in fact, the former. Facing a renown warlord and struggling with a near mutinous army at his side, Alexander was forced to give up and abandon India altogether. He left generals in the already-conquered communities across the north, including the loyal King Porus, but personally headed back to Macedonia via Persia.

The journey home was unexpectedly fruitful, and yet nearly devastating for Alexander of Macedonia. While crossing Punjab, the retreating army, still massive in number, encountered an enemy tribe, the Malli. The Macedonian army attacked with full force against a strong and determined rival, eventually chasing the Malli to their home city. The Citadel, built upon an island within a loop of the Hydraotis River, was precarious and not easy to overtake. During the ensuing siege, Alexander himself was shot through the lung by an enemy arrow. Believing their great leader to be dead, the Macedonians fought bitterly until the city was taken and the Malli crushed under their military might. Indeed alive thanks to the administrations of his personal physician, Philip of Acarnania, Alexander claimed the city and added it to his Indian earnings before moving out with his soldiers, horses, and weaponry. He left his appointed administrators in charge to deal with tribute to the empire and never returned to India or Macedonia, dying only two years later of an unknown illness in Babylon.

With the mighty Macedonian ruler out of the picture, India quickly fell back into the hands of local rulers. It was only 322 BCE, four years after Alexander the Great had entered India from the west, when a new leader emerged to wrest control of the country out of the hands of the Greeks left behind.

Chapter 5 – The Empire of Chandragupta Maurya

The self-appointed savior of India was Chandragupta Maurya, a man whose birth is shrouded in mystery thanks to conflicting historical accounts. Indian historians do agree that at some point in Maurya's youth, he was adopted as a student by the great political philosopher, Vishnugupta, also known as Chanakya. His teachings in politics and warfare helped him take control of the subcontinent and make it possible for his dynastic family to transform India from a land of patchwork political factions into a centralized empire.

Chandragupta Maurya didn't immediately set his sights on the establishment of an empire. As a young man during the time of Alexander's invasion, Maurya was a teacher in Takshasila (Taxila). It was only at the behest of his guru and father figure, Vishnugupta, that Maurya decided to become personally involved in the political landscape of the day. Vishnugupta was outraged at the Macedonian rule imposed upon his fellow compatriots and was rendered all but hopeless after the defeat of warlord King Porus proved existing Indian armies were unable to match Alexander's forces. With the Macedonian army gone, however, Vishnugupta and his protégé sought to immediately rectify the situation.

Maurya and his mentor traveled first to the Nanda Empire to speak with Dhana Nanda, the ruler whose lands were so vast and whose warriors so plentiful that they'd scared away the Macedonian army with mere rumor alone. When Maurya proposed the creation of an alliance between the kingdoms of India as a means of self-protection, however, Nanda refused–he believed himself powerful and resourceful enough to care for his own lands without conceding anything to a weaker ally. Maurya and Vishnugupta were perplexed and frustrated at Nanda's attitude, but soon, the elder of the two was inspired by a new plan: if Nanda couldn't be persuaded to step up and create a unified India, then perhaps his empire should be stolen by someone who took unity seriously.

Thanks to the tutelage of his patron, Maurya was schooled in the art of warfare. By Vishnugupta's side, Maurya raised an army by creating multiple political alliances with other rulers throughout India. Texts such as the *Parishishtaparvan,* which tells the story of his exploits, say that he found a strong ally in King Parvatka of the Himalayas. With a suitable army, the reformers headed to the modern Magadha region to point their swords at Dhana Nanda. Maurya's first efforts were unsuccessful, but he fought on and after a long series of battles managed to finally capture Nanda's capital city of Pataliputra in 322 BCE.

The capture of Pataliputra was the first step in piecing together the powerful Maurya Empire that would last for more than a century and recast India as a unified people. With Nanda under his power, Maurya turned northward to confront the Macedonians left behind by Alexander the Great. It took several years of military campaigning in Punjab and the former Kingdom of Porus to remove the conquering statesmen from their posts and reclaim the northern section of India, and by that time, one of the Macedonian generals had returned to lay claim to the land he'd helped Alexander conquer.

It was General Seleucus who came back to the Indus River Valley following his successful claim to rule Babylon and much of Alexander's adjacent Asian lands. Expecting to find a large tract of land along the river in the hands of his fellow Macedonians, Seleucus instead found himself facing off against the newly born

Mauryan Empire. It was exactly this scenario for which Emperor Maurya and Vishnugupta had been preparing.

Seleucus fought against the armies of Maurya for two years before admitting defeat. He was not content to retreat with nothing, however, and so signed a formal peace treaty with the emperor that was celebrated with the intermarriage between the families of the rulers. The Macedonian princess, one of the daughters of Seleucus (though her name is not certain) was married to Emperor Maurya. She stayed in India, while her father and his army went back to Persia with a gift of 500 war elephants.

Over the course of 139 years of Mauryan rule, the empire created a great deal of wealth by importing and exporting goods to and from China, Sumatra, Persia, Ceylon, and Mediterranean cities. It was the era of the famed Silk Road, an established trade route that linked every major city and port between Constantinople, capital of the Roman Empire in modern Turkey and Beijing, China. By focusing their merchant ventures in local cities along the route, the Mauryan people were able to sell a collection of silks and spices from local producers, as well as exotic items such as rugs, precious metals and stones, perfumes, and fabrics that had been procured from their own travels to nearby regions.

The great emperor grew weary of military life in his old age and stepped down from his role so that he could be succeeded by his son, Bindusara.

Chapter 6 – Buddhism and the Regrets of Ashoka

"If I were asked under what sky the human mind has most fully developed some of its choicest gifts, has most deeply pondered on the greatest problems of life, and has found solutions, I should point to India."

(Max Mueller, *India: What it Can Teach Us*)

Like his grandfather, Chandragupta Maurya, Emperor Ashoka was brought up to follow the Hindu way of life. He read the Vedic texts, schooled his own children in the ceremonies of ancient teachings, and married many women as was the custom of his family and his people. Spiritual beliefs and customs were not something that weighed heavily on the mind of an emperor quick to his sword until a life-changing battle filled him with remorse. It was the Conquest of the Kalingas that forever altered the heart of Emperor Ashoka and the spiritual landscape of India itself.

The Kingdom of Kalinga was located at the southeastern edge of modern India, along the Bay of Bengal. In every direction except east, Kalinga was surrounded by Ashoka's Mauryan Empire and therefore under constant political pressure to submit to the power of the emperor. Since the establishment of the empire by Chandragupta Maurya himself, the purpose of rule was to integrate every corner of the subcontinent under the centralized authority of the emperors, and so, Ashoka was compelled to conquer it. Therefore, soon after he had been recognized as Emperor following the retirement of his father, Ashoka looked to Kalinga and prepared to wage war.

An estimated 150,000 Kalinga warriors and 100,000 Maurya warriors were killed in what has been documented as one of the world's most fierce and bloody clashes. The Daya River, which ran near the battlefield, is said to have been stained red with the blood of the slain soldiers. Of those Kalinga who survived the massacre, most were deported from their land of birth at the command of Emperor Ashoka. The emperor himself had these reports carved over the surfaces of large boulders to commemorate his achievements–and also to document his great lament over having caused such suffering in the name of imperialism. It had indeed been a life-changing experience not only for those subjugated to the Mauryan Empire or sent out of India altogether but for the leader of the winning side. Said Ramesh Prasad Mohapatra in *Military History of Orissa*:

> No war in the history of India is as important either for its intensity or for its results as the Kalinga war of Ashoka. No wars in the annals of the human history has changed the heart of the victor from one of wanton cruelty to that of an exemplary piety as this one. From its fathomless womb the history of the world may find out only a few wars to its credit which may be equal to this war and not a single one that would be greater than this. The political history of mankind is really a history of wars and no war has ended with so successful a mission of the peace for the entire war-torn humanity as the war of Kalinga.

Indeed, once Kalinga fell to Ashoka's forces and was reorganized under the rule of the empire, Emperor Ashoka vowed never again to wage war in order to expand his empire. He had seen destruction, misery, murder, and fear firsthand and was forever changed by it. Known as a bloody and savage ruler beforehand, Emperor Ashoka emerged from the Kalinga War a different ruler. No longer a lapsed

Hindu and a bloodthirsty tyrant, he took up the path of the Buddha as many others in his empire had done. The edicts Ashoka had printed upon stone certify that "After the Kalingas had been conquered, Beloved of the Gods began to feel a strong inclination toward the Dhamma, a love for the Dhamma, and for instruction in Dhamma."

Dhamma, also known in Sanskrit as "Dharma," is difficult to translate into English, though scholars have suggested "piety," "morality," and "righteousness" to stand in its place. Essentially a theoretical construct concerning one's spirituality and lifestyle, Dhamma was proposed by the monk Siddhartha Gautama about two centuries before Emperor Ashoka succeeded to his father's throne. Known afterward simply as the Buddha, Siddhartha Gautama taught a life of peace and tranquility to his followers throughout India, giving light to a new spiritual school, that of Buddhism. Siddhartha's original philosophies and teachings evolved over the centuries, eventually to be summarized into five main abstinences: killing living things, lying, intoxication, sexual misconduct, and stealing. This ethical foundation is which lies at the heart of Dhamma, and they are what inspired Emperor Ashoka to engrave the Major Rock Edicts—the continued documentation of his exploits on a series of boulders—as historical evidence of his enlightened ways.

By the time Ashoka was emperor, Buddhism had been adopted by many Indians who also rejected the use of money, according to their interpretation of Siddhartha's teachings. The wave of Buddhism had also reached many thousands of people in nearby Sri Lanka and Central Asia, with it later spreading to other parts of Asia. Feeling a strong moral obligation to patronize the Indian Buddhism schools, Ashoka invested lavishly in the Buddhist network of monasteries and spiritual leaders. He commissioned great, beautiful temples across his lands at which the many Buddhists of the empire could convene, take refuge, and establish a true, organized religion. The stupas erected by Ashoka were meant to mimic the original burial mounds of the scattered ashes of Buddha. Though these were eventually eroded with time, many of Ashoka's stupas were rebuilt and stand today as a symbol of Buddhism's golden era in India.

With their emperor turning to Dhamma, the people of the Mauryan Empire flocked to their local Buddhist monasteries to claim their own love of Dhamma and begin a new spiritual path. The monasteries were flooded, in fact, so much so that India's Buddhist leaders arranged to host the Third Buddhist Council at Pataliputra, near the Ganges, in 250 BCE; the first reason for the gathering was to address the tens of thousands of new members who held conflicting beliefs or lifestyles to that of the strict Dhamma proposed by its leaders. It seemed that because of the immense influx of wealth suddenly streaming into the temples from none other than the emperor, people all over the empire had decided to join the rich new faith and rejoice in nothing more than its material benefits.

Following the Council, Buddhist leaders in the Maurya Empire and abroad were instructed to question each of their monks personally, so as to ascertain whether he was even familiar with the concepts of Dhamma. Those who had no answers were removed from their posts and monasteries, thus purifying the Buddhist movement of thousands of unqualified members. Emperor Ashoka, for his part, became a true Buddhist ruler in every way he saw fit—he waged no wars for dominance, he stopped his household from eating all but a small quantity of meat, and genuinely tried to meet the basic needs of his subjects. As he inscribed in the Major Rock Edicts, "Whatever exertion I make, I strive only to discharge debt that I owe to all living creatures."

Under the successive kings of Chandragupta Maurya's dynasty, the entire subcontinent was eventually absorbed within the Maurya Empire. Most of the border expansion was due to Chandragupta's grandson, Emperor Ashoka, who is simultaneously remembered as one of India's greatest rulers and one of its most violent. Bindusara and Ashoka were responsible for solidifying the economy of their empire, though through vastly different means. While Bindusara was a largely diplomatic ruler, using pacts and friendly foreign relations to keep borders strong and trade blossoming; Ashoka did so through fear and pillage.

Emperor Ashoka is considered by many to be the greatest ruler in Indian history, not because of his territorial exploits but because he became a different emperor after grief and shame struck him in the heart. It is believed he died of natural causes in 232 BCE.

Chapter 7 – The Return of the Greeks

When Emperor Ashoka died in 232 BCE, he left behind a largely Buddhist empire of some 30 million inhabitants. Having been a pillar of morality and greatness to his people, the emperor's death marked the beginning of a decline in both Buddhism and in the Mauryan Empire. Taxila first seceded from the empire, citing an oppressive taxation regime; it was only the first in a succession of annexed polities and kingdoms to break apart from the vast patchwork empire Chandragupta and his family had pieced together. Half a century after Ashoka's death, around 180 BCE, the last Mauryan Emperor, Brihadnatha, was assassinated by his own general, Pushyamitra Shunga. Thus began the Shunga Empire, an expansive realm of the north part of the subcontinent that existed alongside a series of renewed Greek conquests.

Though India had shaken off Greco-Macedonian rule just a century and a half earlier, Greece and its vast collection of conquered territories had not forgotten about the Asian subcontinent full of fertile farmland and rich material resources. Roman writer Pliny's *Natural History* described one of India's most precious resources in those years:

Coral is as highly valued among the Indians as Indian pearls. It is also found in the Red Sea, but there it is darker in color...Coral-berries are no less valued by Indian men than specimen Indian pearls by Roman ladies. Indian soothsayers and seers believe that coral is potent as a charm for warding off dangers. Accordingly, they delight in its beauty and religious power. Before this became known, the Gauls used to decorate their swords, shields and helmets with coral. Now it is very scarce because of the price it commands, and is rarely seen in its natural habitat.

At its cultural and territorial height of influence in the years after the breakup of the Mauryan Empire, Greece had expanded into a range of Hellenistic kingdoms and territories—so named because of the word Hellas, meaning Greece. These realms stretched south into North Africa and northward from the Mediterranean into Asia. The Greek territories adjacent to India fell under the control of one of Alexander the Great's generals, Seleucus, and remained in Hellenistic control for several generations. This proximity produced the Greco-Bactrian and Indo-Greek kingdoms in the far north of the subcontinent.

India and its adjacent northern neighbors fell under the heavy influence of the Hellenistic conquerors, while the central part of the subcontinent remained united under the leadership of Emperor Shunga. To the far south, the Kingdom of Kalinga had regained its independence from external empires, as did the Pandyan Dynasty and multiple small to mid-sized regions. Here, a cultural divide began to show between the people of the north and the people of the south. The southern Indians were not untouched by the hand of the Greeks, yet they persevered as a culture of mostly Vedic and Hindu people. In the north, religions were plentiful and even faddish in their adoption one after another. The northerners under Asian and Greek rule practiced Buddhism, Hinduism, Jainism, Hellenism, and Zoroastrianism. Since the Greeks had long worshiped multiple gods, their evolving beliefs merged well with those of their Indian, Chinese, and Pakistani colonies.

In eastern central India, Pushyamitra Shunga was a follower of the Vedic god, Lord Shiva, and as such, he put a target on the Buddhists of his realm. Beyond promoting Shiva, Emperor Shunga actively had Buddhists killed to purify his monotheistic beliefs; it is perhaps due to this blatant form of ethnic cleansing that Buddhism shrank so significantly out of favor in most of India. Shunga was just as dedicated to warfare for the sake of territorial gain as Ashoka had been against it, and through a series of battles he took about one-third of the total land India and adjacent regions had to offer.

Though Shunga and his nine dynastic successors were quick to the sword, theirs was a period of Indian history in which the arts and education grew. It was through royal Shunga patronage that literature, architecture, and the pursuit of higher education and artistic pursuits was achievable for citizens of the empire. The archaeological record of that period, from about 184 BCE to 73 BCE, includes a variety of finely detailed jewelry, small terra-cotta sculptures, large sculptures, tablets, and architectural monuments. The latter includes the chaitya hall at Bhaja and the renowned Great Stupa at Sanchi. Though the first Emperor Shunga murdered Buddhists outright, later dynastic rulers took a more reverent attitude toward those members of the peaceful faith, repairing the monuments of Ashoka respectfully.

Like the early art of the Vedics, Shunga art features many-limbed gods in symbolic dress and pose. It's easy to see how the dominant successor to the Maurya Empire protected much of future India from the changes wrought by Greek cities and kingdoms in the north, primarily in terms of religion. During this period, Hinduism reigned among the many religious and spiritual paths that characterized that part of the world, so much so that it ceased to be considered a religion so much as it was a way of living to honor the traditions of one's predecessors.

Both the north and south of India were affected economically by the Greek presence in the Middle East, and the whole of the subcontinent used coins struck from a variety of fine metals, including copper and gold. The northern varieties were usually round as per the Greek standard; those in the south retained their classical Indian features and were usually square. The coins featured Hellenistic emperors and Hindu gods, two languages, Greek and Sanskrit. These were used in trade not only within the Greco-Indian kingdoms but also as far away as China.

In approximately 125 BCE, the Greco-Indian constructs were partially conquered by Scythians from eastern regions of Asia. This caused the Greeks to abandon Bactria and move farther south into central India. By the 1st century CE, the Yuezhi tribes of China established the Kushan Empire in what had once been Indo-Greek and Greco-Bactrian strongholds. Once more, the Greeks were removed from the subcontinent—and this time, they would not return.

Chapter 8 – The Gupta Empire

In the 4th century CE, a new ruler arose with a rather familiar name: Chandragupta. Like his namesake from centuries gone by, Chandragupta I was the first emperor of his dynasty and the leader of an empire that would flourish for more than 200 years. At the height of its reach, the Gupta Empire encompassed nearly all of modern northeast India, from Punjab to Kamarupa.

Like their ancestors, the Gupta rulers annexed the bulk of their empire through warfare; however, the vast region under their control enjoyed relative peace and security. Under the Guptas, this section of India underwent a golden age during which the arts once more came to the forefront of civilian life. Though the rulers were Hindu themselves, they were tolerant of followers of Buddhism and Jainism. Nevertheless, the Gupta Empire was a nation of more than one culture, though all those encompassed within it are classically considered Indian. There were the original Indus Valley people, the Aryans, and families with Greek or Chinese heritage living together under the shelter of the Himalayas. In such conditions, scholarly pursuit thrived.

A Buddhist university was established at Nalanda, in the northeastern part of the country near the very mountains where

Buddhist temples dot the valleys between peaks even now. The school stood as a proud reminder of India's Buddhist roots, even in the wake of the violent and singular Shunga Dynasty. Nalanda attracted intellects from near and far, both within the Gupta Empire and from Tibet, Nepal, China, Korea, and other Asian civilizations who wanted to study a specialized form of Buddhism: Mahayana. This particular school of Buddhism is probably purely Indian in its origins since it is usually believed to have been conceived within India.

Buddhists who follow the Mahayana path seek enlightenment specifically for the betterment of all beings. The writings of Mahayana Buddhists insist that the ultimate goal of reaching total enlightenment can be achieved within one lifetime (Buddhists believe in the possibility of more than one lifetime) and by anyone who commits to living according to Dhamma.

Now, I, Vairocana Buddha

Am sitting atop a lotus pedestal;

On a thousand flowers surrounding me

Are a thousand Sakyamuni Buddhas.

Each flower supports a hundred million worlds;

In each world a Sakyamuni Buddha appears.

All are seated beneath a Bodhi-tree,

All simultaneously attain Buddhahood.

All these innumerable Buddhas

Have Vairocana as their original body.

These countless Sakyamuni Buddhas

All bring followers along -- as numerous as

motes of dust.

(translation of the *Brahma Net Sutra*)

The concept of enlightenment, in terms of Buddhism, relates to total spiritual knowledge. According to the original Buddha, it is the ultimate wisdom. One of the facets of this understanding is called "Tuka," the existence of suffering and things that are finite. The second facet of enlightenment is understanding why each of these sufferings come about. To followers of any Buddhist school of thought, each birth, suffering, and death serves a purpose. The third facet of enlightenment is the cessation of suffering, which includes the end of death. Finally, enlightenment includes the knowledge of how to end suffering.

Buddha believed that as humans, we are caught up in the false reality of material things, superficial relationships with objects, and other people. Instead of giving in to cravings for objects, the teachers and students at Nalanda taught that the way to enlightenment was to look past instinctual desires. For these purposes, Buddhists in the Gupta Empire focused on mindfulness, meditation, and minimalism. In terms of the five main abstinences of the religion, enlightenment can be measured by how little you are affected by a life free of stealing, sexual misconduct, lying, intoxication, and killing living creatures.

Education in the Gupta Empire was not just isolated to the Buddhist teachings at Nalanda, however. The Hindu alternative to Nalanda and the Buddhist monasteries of the day were Brahmanical Agraharas, where the subjects of the Vedic texts and subsects like Ayurveda were taught. Ayurveda translates into "The Science of Life," and it relates predominantly to food and medicine. Ayurveda aims to explain and help treat human ailments using food, meditation, and other regimes by balancing the humors of the body: earth, air, fire, water, and ether. Each type of food that potentially makes up one's diet, from the humble lentil to a leg of lamb, is documented carefully in terms of its health benefits and possible negative influences. Ayurveda, as a subsect of the major Hindu Vedas, is still very much in practice today.

The Agraharas that taught such knowledge were built on pieces of land bequeathed to keepers of the Hindu faith—known as

Brahmans—who in return would maintain temples and religious sites on the land. These sites were often used as pilgrimage locations for people seeking higher spiritual knowledge from the Vedas. The costs of upkeep on the Agraharas were incurred by the royal Gupta family.

In addition to religious and spiritual learning, universities like the one at Taxila offered lessons in astronomy, mathematics, science, accounting, politics, law, arts, and architecture. It was a period of beautiful, intricate stone carvings, rock-etched architecture, and lifelike sculptures that makes up India's Classical period artworks. Realistic renderings of the Vishnu, Shiva, and Buddha were crafted in paint, which can be found in the Ajanta Caves, as well as in stone, like the massive three-headed god at the Elephanta Caves. Rock-cut caves, dwellings, and public buildings are more plentiful in India than in any other part of the world, thanks to the incredible work of the pioneering builders of the Maurya Empire and then the determined perfectionists of Gupta-era architects

To create a rock-cut structure, the stone mason had to select an appropriately sized outcropping of solid rock, usually sandstone or in some cases marble. Masons also used the basalt hills of the Sahyadri mountain range in the western part of the country. It is believed that the first rock-cut caves carved out by early Indian builders were meant to mimic the darkness, isolation, and solitude of natural caves since the latter were revered by religious sects who used them to pray. By the Gupta era, cave building had been perfected and expanded to include massive rock-cut temples. These are a stunning sight to behold, rich in ornamental detail and large enough in scale to rival any free-standing structure of the age. From the humblest of caves—complete with carved, peaked archways and polished flat walls—to the highly intricate Mahabodhi Temple in Bodh Gaya, it is largely from works created during those centuries of Gupta reign that we can see the coming together of a unified style of Indian architecture.

The Gupta dynasty grew in terms of territory following the reign of Chandragupta I, succeeding into the hands of family members for nearly a century and a half until the Huns, a nomadic Asian tribe, invaded in the latter part of the 5th century. Fundamentally weakened, Gupta kings persisted in governing their small remaining lands, but ultimately, the empire faded out of existence after 550 CE. Dozens of rock-cut caves from this time can still be visited today.

Chapter 9 – Ancient Mathematical Discoveries

"We owe a lot to the Indians, who taught us how to count, without which no worthwhile scientific discovery could have been made."

(Albert Einstein)

Great building knowledge did not come without a solid understanding of geometry and mathematical concepts. By the 3rd century CE, Indians had begun using a decimal number system to express large values that may have been introduced by Chinese traders. The local origins of this system are unclear, but what's certain is that Indian mathematicians revolutionized the practice of using numbers from the third to fifth centuries. In fact, they created a set of numerals to use for the values 1 through 9 that would become the basis for counting and mathematics the world over. This set of numerals is credited to Aryabhata in the 5th or 6th century CE. We still use this Hindu-Arabic system today, regardless of regional language differences, making mathematics a truly universal language that spans nations.

Aryabhata also approximated the Pi ratio to within four decimal places. In doing so, he realized it was an irrational number, meaning that any calculation in which it was used could only be an approximation at best. Nevertheless, he saw the potential of the Pi approximation and used it to calculate the circumference of the earth to within 113 kilometers (70 miles) of the actual circumference. These calculations would be incredibly important for the future of mathematics and astronomy.

The mathematician also realized that he could arrange equations so that those with more than one missing value could be solved. This was particularly useful in working with right triangles, thanks to the sine function. Using sine—a specific ratio of sides of a right triangle that describe the precise measurement of acute angles—Aryabhata was able to disprove astronomers who proposed that the moon was farther from the earth than the sun. The proof was in the angles. If two individuals view the sun from different locations, they can gather enough information to create a triangular representation of their lookout positions and the sun. It can be shown this way (though not to scale):

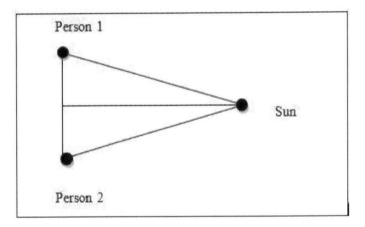

So, if a simplistic star chart were to be drawn of the surrounding fixed points in the sky—like the moon or Venus, for example—each person observing the sun must mark the observed position of the sun. If the observers are 10 meters apart, there will be a ten-meter disconnect in their recorded object locations relative to the other markers in the star chart. Therefore, a new triangle is formed as if the first has been flipped over, leaving the sun at the same spot.

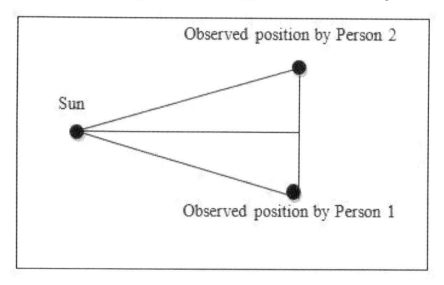

The distance between the observers and their respective observed positions of the sun is the same. Since the calculation must be performed on a right triangle, the model is split in half, making the shortest line of the triangle only half the distance that was initially between the two observers. Using a secondary calculation, astronomers can find the precise angular measurement for that most acute angle, then use the sine ratio to determine the length of the other two lines. Therefore, the sun and the earth are separated by nearly 150 million kilometers, or 93 million miles.

Aryabhata was by no means the only mathematical innovator to come from India. Another important contributor to the field was Brahmagupta, an Indian astronomer and mathematician of the 7th century. His work is evidenced deep inside the sandstone city of Fort

Gwalior in central India where archaeologists found the first written proof of what was perhaps India's greatest addition to mathematics: the zero. Probably in use since the 5th century, the concept of zero was a difficult one to grasp for even the brightest minds of the age—and yet it was a digit without which the numeric system was incomplete. Historians place the concise development of this humble digit on Brahmagupta.

Brahmagupta forged the fundamental rules of the use of zero within mathematical calculations, which was significant because until that time it had merely been used as a placeholder within larger numbers. According to these rules, $1+0=1$; $1-0=1$; and $1x0=0$. Now, large calculations could be carried out easily, be they addition, subtraction, or multiplication. Yet, one of the rules of zero evaded Brahmagupta: that of its division. This puzzle would not be completed for several more centuries, but the works of India's most renowned mathematician had already changed the face of the pursuit of everything from simple pastoral accounting to complex trigonometry and algebra needed for astronomy.

Working further with zeros, Indian mathematicians, Brahmagupta included, discovered a completely hypothetical way to use digits: negative numbers. It was a whole new perspective on math, in that numbers could be used to represent potential values. The first use of negative numbers was to represent debts on accounting sheets. For example, if a customer ordered and paid for six swatches of silk from a merchant, then left with only four, the current value of swatch numbers sits at -2 in favor of the customer. If he or she takes four and pays for 2, it's -2 in favor of the merchant. Negative numbers and their wider use in mathematics wouldn't be fully examined in Europe for another 1,000 years, but Brahmagupta worked with them extensively.

He also worked with positive numbers—specifically, distances and physical measurements—to further develop the Greeks' written language of trigonometry. He published several works in which he criticized his fellow astronomers for using faulty methodology and lay the groundwork for various types of mathematics, including algebra, geometry, and trigonometry. Within the latter field, he described a formula for working out the area of a cyclic quadrilateral—that is a four-sided figure with all four vertices (corners) on the circumference of the circle. Brahmagupta's formula is written as follows, where K is the area of the quadrilateral and a, b, c, and d are lengths of the figure's sides.

$$K = \frac{1}{4} \sqrt{(-a+b+c+d)(a-b+c+d)(a+b-c+d)(a+b+c-d)}$$

Brahmagupta and Aryabhata's work was founded on the mathematical calculations of the early Greeks, but they managed more precise calculations than those of their predecessors. Much of the same methodology they invented would not be discovered and used in Europe until the 17th century.

Chapter 10 – The Delhi Sultanate

The next period of Indian history centered on the exploits of the Turk, Qutb al-Dīn Aibak. By Aibak's lifetime in the 12th century CE, Islam had become a distinct culture within India through simple migration. Though some land disputes and clashes had taken place on a small scale, it was not until the 11th century CE that members of Islam decided on a political tactic of complete Indian subjugation under the great and powerful Persian Empire.

Born in Turkistan, Aibak was sold into slavery to a Persian who took him away from his homeland as a child. In Persia, he served a succession of important masters that eventually included the Sultan of the Ghorid Empire. Evidently a trustworthy and clever bondsman, Aibak was granted the title of Master of Slave by the sultan himself. Proving himself more than capable of such administration, Aibak was ultimately appointed to the high office of military general for the sultan's army, which had been tasked with the conquest of the Indian city of Delhi. Thus, Qutb al-Dīn Aibak found himself in India around the year 1193.

Delhi did indeed fall to the Ghorid army, after which the sultan returned home and left the administration of the city and other conquered north Indian lands to Aibak. Happy with his charge,

Aibak continued to add more regions of India to the Ghorid territories until his master was assassinated in 1206. Seeing his opportunity to become the unquestioned ruler of the lands he had been integral in obtaining, Aibak married the heir of his only political rival in Persia and declared himself the Sultan of Delhi.

Qutb al-Dīn Aibak died only four years after having established his kingdom, but the lands he'd annexed in India and adjacent regions remained united under a succession of sultans. The Delhi Sultanate, as it came to be known, had only penetrated into the utmost northern region of modern India and also contained lands within Bangladesh, Pakistan, Nepal, and Bhutan. The first to rule this kingdom after Aibak—one of his own sons—was quickly murdered by the deceased sultan's son-in-law, Shams ud-Din Iltutmish, who took the leadership role for himself. This was the beginning of the Slave (or Mamluk) Dynasty, the first of five Delhi-based dynasties governed by a series of sultans of Turkic origin.

The entire Delhi Sultanate, as this collection of dynasties is called, spanned more than 300 years between 1206 to 1526. Thus, Turks essentially kept control of the majority of the subcontinent throughout India's Middle Ages, with Persian functioning as their common language.

One of the most notable sultans of this particular dynasty was Razia Sultana, the only female to hold such a title during the entire three-century span of the Delhi Sultanate. A granddaughter of Qutb al-Dīn Aibak, Razia was a favorite child of her father, Iltutmish, and the latter granted her power of succession when her eldest brother died. Being a sultan was not an easy role for a woman due to the hatred Razia faced from the men in her own army and among her own brothers.

The Sultanate was a purely patriarchal society, and Razia's rise to the throne was completely unprecedented. To try to overcome the negativity, Razia dressed in the clothes of a man while leading the army to confront her usurper brother, Muiz ud-Din Bahram, in Delhi in 1240. She was killed by her own turncoat military generals who had been loath to follow the commands of a woman.

In 1290, Jalal-ud-din Khalji established the successor to the Slave Dynasty: the Khalji Dynasty. By this time, the kingdom stretched all the way westward to the Arabian Sea and almost down to the southernmost tip of the subcontinent. Further conquest was not the most pressing issue facing the sultans of the Khalji Dynasty, however, since they were busy keeping the Mongols out of their territory. Under the leadership of Genghis Khan, the fearsome Mongol army began to forcefully press its way through China, Afghanistan, and the Turkic countries of the Middle East. Repeatedly, Khan's and eventually his successor's armies tried to vanquish India, but the vast lands of the Sultanate remained untouched by Mongol hordes—except for a portion of Punjab. The attacks began in 1222 and did not cease until 1327.

The constant need for military might during that century all but exhausted the Sultanate's resources. Sultan Alauddin Khalji, therefore, completely reorganized the kingdom's taxation system in the early 14th century, raising agriculture taxes from 20 percent to 50 percent and cutting the salaries of administrative officials. He was also forced to cut the salaries of government-sponsored poets and scholars. In addition to these measures, Alauddin placed a heavy financial burden on the members of his kingdom who did not conform to his religion, Islam.

Under the new laws, non-Muslims were expected to pay a total of four new taxes: land, house, pasture, and poll. Essentially, this meant that each non-Muslim male adult in the Sultanate was required to pay an annual fee for residing within the sultan's lands: for owning a house, for owning and tending pastures, and for owning any sort of lands. These measures were not only for financial reasons, though they served to vastly reduce the debts of the Sultanate; they were meant to effectively wear down the millions of Hindus in the land until the people were simply too impoverished to organize a rebellion.

Sultan Alauddin Khalji didn't stop at taxation reform. Next, he reorganized market laws that were meant to take effect throughout the Sultanate but possibly only were enforced in the capital. These changes included price fixes for basic goods like grain, animals, slaves, and textiles. In addition, hoarding was made illegal, and those found guilty of such were punished violently.

The more extreme of Alauddin's reforms—notably the market changes—were repealed by his successor, but his methods of extracting funds through taxation of the lower classes remained a keystone in the future administration of empires. In 1320, many of these taxes were still in place when Ghiyath al-Din Tughluq took his place as the first sultan of the Tughlaq Dynasty. Under Tughlaq's instruction, the Sultanate's military regime marched on, annexing almost every piece of the subcontinent except for the stubborn region around Kalinga.

Hungry for territory and ever-increasing power, Sultan Tughluq was renown as a hot-headed and vicious leader. He also had a lavish habit of expecting gifts from visitors, which he would return in kind. In this manner, a clever Moroccan traveler called Ibn Battuta secured for himself a furnished home, thousands of silver pieces of currency and a job collecting taxes from Hindu villages. In Battuta's memoirs, he noted the extremism to which his patron was inclined.

> Not a week passed without the spilling of much Muslim blood and the running of streams of gore before the entrance of his palace. This included cutting people in half, skinning them alive, chopping off heads and displaying them on poles as a warning to others, or having prisoners tossed about by elephants with swords attached to their tusks.

Battle was not the only brutality faced by members of the Sultanate; slavery was also rampant during the Tughlaq Dynasty. Though it had been practiced since the Sultanate was founded, ironically by an ex-slave, it flourished under Tughlaq. He patronized a slave trading market in which Indian and foreign slaves were brought to be sold, and he even made gifts of slaves to foreign rulers for diplomatic purposes. Because his regime was so strict, much of the territorial gain made by Sultan Tughlaq dissolved after his death. The Sayyid Dynasty replaced that of the Tughlaq in 1414, only to last a brief 37 years. The last Sayyid ruler, Alam Shah, surrendered Delhi to Bahlul Lodi in 1451, beginning the Lodi Dynasty.

The last chapter of the Delhi Sultanate lasted for 75 years, during which time multiple competing sultanates were annexed and new cities built. Sultan Sikandar Lodi founded the city of Agra in 1504 and made this the new capital of the kingdom. He also removed taxes on corn, enforced taxation audits on members of the nobility, and commissioned the translation of Sanskrit medical texts into Persian. Due to his religious fervor, many Muslim mosques were built and maintained within the borders of his Sultanate.

Lodi's son and heir was the last of the Delhi Sultans, and he was killed at the Battle of Panipat, attempting to save his Sultanate from the encroaching Mughal Empire. The year was 1526.

Chapter 11 – Babur and the Mughal Empire

Sultan Lodi's final enemy went by the name of Babur, and like the rulers of the ruined Sultanate, Babur's heritage was central Asian—specifically, the Timurid Empire. A descendent of Emperor Timur, and possibly even of Genghis Khan, Babur had a royal lineage and a strong desire to establish his own empire. When Sultan Lodi passed, he got his chance to rule over most of India as ruler of the Mughal Empire.

It is somewhat ironic to note that for as much money and military might Alauddin and his family spent keeping the Mongols out of India, it ultimately fell under the command of a Mongol descendent just the same. In fact, the word "Mughal" is most likely a derivation of the original word "Mongol." For India's Hindus, Buddhists, and Jains, little changed, since Babur was a Muslim ruler just as had been the Sultanates.

Babur's people, descended from the Mongol hordes of Genghis Khan, were covetous of a vast country that boasted the world's only known diamond mines, an enticing array of food and spice, and 120 million people who knew how to farm, excavate, spin and weave textiles, build, care for livestock, and create priceless jewelry. They also knew how to fight for their leader, a trait that the Mughal Babur very much wanted to exploit for himself.

It took twenty years and many attempts for the Mughals to penetrate Muslim India, but in 1525 he decided to focus his energy—and that of his relatively sparse army of 12,000—on the powerful city of Delhi. He rode with his troops westward, intent on making this campaign successful. His first move was to lay a trap for the city's skilled leader and protector, Sultan Ibrahim Lodi. The ambush was set at Panipat, a community just a few miles from the city.

Babur settled easily into Panipat with his warriors, knowing that once the Sultan heard of his presence, the latter would ride out to meet him at the head of his defending army. This was a tactic often used in India and throughout Europe by tribal rulers and emperors, intended to allow the heads of opposing forces to discuss potential diplomatic terms. The Mughal conqueror was counting on his enemy following this particular code of conduct, but he didn't plan on reciprocating any such protocol of war. Instead, he ordered his soldiers to dig a trench on one side of Panipat that effectively forced approaching riders into a tightening funnel—delivering them in a tight formation to the Mughal warriors, waiting with composite bow and arrows at the ready. They also brought a high-tech and terrifying weapon along for this particular campaign: the cannon.

Sultan Ibrahim Lodi met the Mughal army on April 21st, 1526, fully prepared for war. He brought with him 40,000 soldiers and 1,000 elephants, and stampeded directly into the prepared funnel, unaware until it was too late to pull back and attack from another direction. Babur's forces shot the oncoming army with a crash of cannon fire, terrorizing the elephants and causing chaos for Lodi's side. Frightened, the elephants tried to stampede away, crushing and killing many of their human companions. With backup from the long-range archers, Babur astonishingly and quite easily overcame the Sultan's attack, killing Lodi and tens of thousands of his soldiers before the battle was over.

Delhi's protectors dealt with, Babur moved into the city with his troops and found it just as he'd imagined: luxurious and full of unprecedented wealth. With the resources of Delhi in hand, there was nothing he couldn't achieve in outlying India. There was money to pay for loyalty, and it was spent lavishly. Though his troops wanted to take their spoils of war and return to the cooler plains of their homelands, Babur had other ideas. He wanted to do something unusual for a man of his culture: put down roots.

To facilitate his own permanence in India, Babur continued with his army down the length of the Himalayas until he'd conquered every city from Delhi to Patna. Each independent kingdom or principality was consolidated into the burgeoning Mughal Empire as Babur and his architects physically put their mark on the cityscapes. For a civilization of fearsome conquerors, Babur's people were incredibly adept at construction and architectural design. They loved water features, crafting waterworks so intricate that a seemingly level body of water would function practically to feed a fountain many meters away. In the lovely water gardens, crafted from stone, Babur and his advisors would hold political meetings and entertain important guests.

The Mughals were a technologically advanced civilization, not only in terms of architecture but also their metalworking. The swords used by Babur and his armies to conquer India were forged from Damascus steel, a metal that could stay sharp and hold a strong edge for longer than any other metal in the known world. Specialist blacksmiths worked for hours on each blade, layering sheets of steel together and forming a strong composite of high-carbon and low-carbon veneers. From this material, they created swords, knives, shields, spears, bows, arrowheads, cannons, and early types of handguns called matchlocks, blunderbusses, and flintlocks. Even their war elephants were equipped with steel blades, crafted to fit over the sawed-off stump of their tusks. Truly, theirs was a society built on the conquest and defense of warfare.

Elephant training was a very serious business to Babur and his military peers. Not only were the 2,000- to 5,000-kilogram (4,400- to 11,000-pound) elephants taught to trample the enemy beneath their immense feet, but Mughal officers trained the giant animals to use their bladed tusks in tandem with their agile trunks, effectively grabbing and ripping the enemy to pieces. Contemporary artists depict these elephants as confident killing machines, dressed with blades and protected by vast blankets of quilted leather or steel that sat up behind the head to protect the driver.

As Emperor Babur furthered his conquest of India, he brought hundreds of elephants that were trained in warfare and as confident in battle as the most experienced human soldier. The elephants were feared far and wide, featured in gruesome, full-color artworks in full armor with bloodied tusks and appendages, purposefully slicing through legions of enemy soldiers. A watercolor illustration attributed to the 16th-century artists Basawan and Chetar shows Akbar riding an elephant in pursuit of an enemy, another elephant by their side. They were an incredibly important part of Mughal warfare, ceremony, and overall culture—and would remain so throughout the ages in India.

In addition to artists, and the Persian language, the Mughal's brought a love of beauty that would physically change the urban cityscapes and become part of India's eternal identity.

Chapter 12 – The Taj Mahal and a Story of Love

Babur's kingdom passed to his son Humayun, who at his death bestowed it upon his own son Jahangir. When Jahangir breathed his last, his four sons fought over the succession until Shah Jahan, born in January of 1592, murdered his brother, cousins, and all male rivals for his father's throne. He became the emperor in 1628, at the age of 36. It was an incongruous beginning to the rule of the Mughal Emperor who would actually be remembered for his tender love story. Today, Shah Jahan's monument of love, the Taj Mahal, is visited by 60,000 people every day.

Shah Jahan's love story began long before he gained power; it happened at the age of 15 in the marketplace of Agra. There, he saw a beautiful girl whose presence filled him with desire and adoration. The two fell in love instantly, and a marriage was planned. Though they were forced to wait five years for the wedding to take place, their feelings did not waver, nor did they question the powerful emotions that had overtaken them upon meeting.

In true Mughal style, Shah Jahan was both bloodthirsty in battle and quite intellectual in politics. He adored architecture and set about building beautiful palaces throughout his kingdom that were crafted of brilliant white marble. They would come to further define the urban landscape of India, Pakistan, Afghanistan, and many south Asian and Middle Eastern countries, as well as the Muslim faith itself. Jahan knew that it was both his right and in his faith's tradition that he marry more than one woman. While he waited for the far-off date his astrologers proposed for the wedding to Mumtaz Mahal, Jahan chose another bride to marry right away. At the age of 20, Shah Jahan married his first choice and eventually became husband to three women. Upon the final marital union in 1612, the newlyweds embarked upon their life together with gusto.

Mumtaz Mahal was not just a lovely trinket for her husband to admire. Though Shah Jahan showered her with gifts, he also treasured their friendship and her wisdom. The couple sought counsel from one another as well as tenderness. On March 23rd, 1614, the empress gave birth to their first child, a daughter named Jahanara Begum. The next year, they welcomed a prince to the family and called him Dara Shikoh. These were just the first of 14 children the royal couple would have together, though, as was normal for this time in history, only seven of the babies would survive to become adults. Still, the family was large and promising.

Though Shah Jahan was his father's preferred successor—indeed, his name meant "King of the World"—the prince still found it necessary to wrench control of the empire from his male family members after the death of his royal father. Once the deed had been done, Jahan and Mahal set to the administration of the realm in earnest. Like his predecessors, Shah Jahan was a devout Muslim who believed in the existence of one God, Allah. Despite his personal ties to Islam, however, Shah Jahan wanted to rule over a kingdom in which he was not only respected but loved by his people. To that end, he declared that Hindus and Muslims were equal in the Mughal Empire, and he even introduced a brand-new language—

Hindavi, also known as Hindustani—to his courts and official offices. A mixture of Sanskrit and Persian, Hindavi allowed members of both religions to converse more easily. This would eventually develop into the modern Hindi and Urdu languages.

The Shah's happiness did not last forever as his favorite empress would not live long past the delivery of her 14th child. As she succumbed to complications from the birth, Shah Jahan promised to build her the most beautiful mausoleum in all creation. She died in 1631, at the age of 38, and left her husband grieving terribly.

According to the famous story, "The king cried out with grief like an ocean raging with storm. He put aside his royal robes and for the whole week afterward, his majesty did not appear in public, nor transact any affairs of state. From constant weeping, he was forced to use spectacles and his hair turned gray."

Six months after his most beloved wife's passing, Shah Jahan ordered a stunning new building to be constructed for Mumtaz Mahal. Like the beautiful waterworks and temples commissioned by his great-grandfather and grandfather, Akbar the Great, the mausoleum was to be immaculate and grand. To meet his exacting taste, however, it and all other palaces under his construction were to be pieced together with only the finest of white marble. The foundations for this great work were laid within sight of his palace in Agra.

For 11 years, white marble was mined in Rajasthan, while red sandstone was shipped from Delhi to meet the demands of the giant tomb. The supplies were brought into Agra on a single-purpose, 16-kilometer (10-mile) ramp, while around the budding tomb, a whole city sprouted to house the 20,000 laborers and artisans working on the project. By 1643, the main mausoleum was complete, but work on the outer grounds continued for another decade. Finished entirely by 1653, the structure sat proudly framed by four thin towers of white stone. Upon the approach, there was a vast, shallow pool. The main building was roofed by a series of Persian domes and studded with archways. Everything appeared serene, peaceful, magnificent, and dazzlingly white. Shah Jahan had fulfilled his promise to house the empress in the greatest monument the world had ever seen.

In addition to the mausoleum itself, the emperor had two more edifices constructed, both in line with the central structure and each facing it from the west and east. From the west lay a mosque; from the east, a rest house. These are of great significance to both the deceased empress and her husband since Islamic tradition states that women who die in childbirth are martyrs. Therefore, their resting places become locations of pilgrimage for the devout near and far. In anticipation of these visitors, Shah Jahan prepared a church in which they could pray and a space in which they could rest from their long and tedious journeys. The guest house, called a mehmaan khana, was a formal nod to the Indian tradition of entertaining travelers and guests in comfortable, amicable accommodations.

Shah Jahan died at the age of 74 in 1666, having lost his lust for leadership and suffered the usurpation of the throne by his son, Aurangzeb. His body was interred next to that of his first love, the Empress Mumtaz Mahal, in the splendid mausoleum he had built for her.

Chapter 13 – India is "Rediscovered" by Portugal

Though India and the Roman Empire had been in contact as early as 30 BCE, the fall of the latter civilization meant that the European world shrank significantly in terms of worldview. The Dark Ages were set in motion, and until the Renaissance of the 14th to 17th centuries, contact between Europe and India was all but lost. For Portugal, recovering its strength and wealth was a feat dedicated to shipbuilding and exploration. In 1498, Vasco da Gama and his crew arrived near modern Calicut and once more connected the Western world to that of India. They were the first post-Greco-Roman European nation to establish a link with India via the Malabar Coast and King Zamorin of Calicut.

Though Portugal beat the rest of Europe to India, it was just one more foreign power among many Asian and Middle Eastern nations already trading with the various empires and kingdoms of pre-Modern India. King Zamorin was friendly to exotic nations and he allowed da Gama to fill his ship with the same aromatic spices that were always in demand of his people. Upon returning to Portugal, the explorer found that these goods were valued at more than sixty times the cost of the entire expedition to India. Once such goods were discovered, there was no doubt about whether more ships would be sent. Over the next years, Portuguese merchants came in droves to Calicut. Their motives were generally selfish, which led them into multiple skirmishes with the local culture and other expatriate traders.

The major source of conflict between Indian nationals and the Portuguese settlers was religion. Portugal was a strictly Catholic country, and India was a land of many gods. The 100 million people who called the subcontinent home were mainly Muslim and Hindu, with significant populations of Jains and Buddhists. Though the Catholic Church was not impressed by any of these belief systems, it took the most offense to Islam which shared an ancient belief in the prophecies of the angel Gabriel. Since the Mughals were faithful to the Islamic church, Portugal was constantly at odds with the Mughal rulers and administrators of the realm; even following several peace treaties and alliances with Indian leaders, Vasco da Gama and his compatriots essentially fought their way up the coast, one moment making alliances and the next breaking them. It was a treacherous and chaotic time for India, with very little pretense that the Portuguese meant to act in the best interests of their hosts.

> A bare two years after Vasco da Gama's voyage a Portuguese fleet led by Pedro Alvarez Cabral arrived on the Malabar coast. Cabral delivered a letter from the king of Portugal to the Samudri (Samudra-raja or Sea-king), the Hindu ruler of the city-state of Calicut, demanding that he expel all Muslims from his kingdom as they were enemies of the 'Holy Faith'. He met with a blank refusal; then afterwards the Samudra steadfastly maintained that Calicut had always been open to everyone who wished to trade there…
>
> (Amitav Ghosh, *In an Antique Land.*)

By 1501, Portugal had obtained the right to maintain a trading depot at Calicut, having signed a friendship agreement with Zamorin. Despite promises to remain peaceful, the Portuguese traders were constantly at odds with the Muslim merchants, oftentimes engaging them in full battle at sea. Just one year after the trading depot was built, da Gama himself returned to Calicut, intent on taking the entire port city for Portugal. He and his troops caused immense damage to the city in the attempt, after which da Gama fled up the coast to find allies among other Indian leaders. Along the way, he set up Portugal's first trading station on the subcontinent at Kochi.

Quickly, the Portuguese worked their way into the southwestern part of India, building factories, trading depots, and small colonies. Several years after da Gama's first voyage to Calicut, they established Portuguese India, a state in the Portuguese Overseas Empire. The capital of that colonial state eventually became Goa, a tiny region in the southwest. Native Goans, as well as the growing community of Portuguese, fell under the political and religious subjugation of the Portuguese crown, some 8,000 kilometers (5,000 miles) away.

This connection meant that Goa was not immune to the strict Portuguese Inquisition, during which time any behavior seen as heretical against the Catholic Church was punished severely. The Inquisition was a formative feature of Catholic Europe during the Medieval period, and in Portugal, it was formally put into law in 1536 at the request of King John III. In Goa, the Inquisition began in 1560 and targeted Jews, Buddhists, Muslims, Hindus and even subsects of Christianity that were deemed inappropriate. Even newly baptized Catholics were chastised under the regime, accused of having switched religions only for political security while continuing to practice their true religion in secret. This was usually referred to as "crypto-Hinduism."

Insisting that Catholicism was the one true faith, Catholic missionaries made sure to burn all books they found written in indigenous languages, including Sanskrit, Arabic, Konkani, and

Marathi. In addition, imported books on Protestant Christianity—a movement gaining popularity in Europe—were strictly banned. All the most horrific legislation that was employed in Europe was mimicked in India. Those people found guilty of heresy were fined, publicly flogged, deported to Mozambique, imprisoned, burned in effigy, or burned at the stake. Though anyone stepping up as a witness at the heresy trials was given anonymity, there was very little an accused person could do to prove their innocence. Their confessions were extracted under torture, and if they recanted, it only served to incriminate them further as evidence of poor character.

When a person was convicted of heresy by the Goan Inquisition, their possessions were appropriated by the state and any religious paraphernalia was destroyed. In addition to personal possessions, Portugal stole public lands on which temples and religious structures were erected, then razed them all to the ground. In all, at least 760 Hindu temples were destroyed over the course of the Inquisition, and Hindus were forced to attend Catholic church services regularly to hear their own belief systems ridiculed. In 1620, it was made illegal for Hindus to perform their own marriage ceremonies.

As the accusation, punishments, and public book burnings continued, Hindus gathered what remained of their sacred objects and fled the state. Goa would remain under Portuguese rule for more than four centuries after the establishment of the Goan Inquistion.

Chapter 14 – The Maratha Empire

Since the conquest of Arabs and Persians in sections of the country from about the 11th century, Islam had been an increasingly important part of the cultural landscape, but that wasn't India's first brush with Muslim people. As early as the 7th century, Muslim traders and immigrants had been part of the land. Cheraman Juma, believed to have been the very first Islamic mosque in India, was built in 629 CE.

Believers in the Prophet Muhammad, Muslims brought their own holy book, the Quran, with them to India. The holy text spoke of the Five Pillars of Islam: the only God is Allah, and his last messenger on Earth was Muhammad; pray five times a day while facing the holy city of Mecca; those with adequate means must give to the poor; Muslims must fast during the ninth month of the year, Ramadan; and those who are able to visit Mecca must do so in the twelfth month of the year.

India was a land of diverse religious beliefs—including various Hindu sects, Buddhism, Jainism, and Sikhism—and therefore, peaceful Muslim traders were perfectly welcome among them. In a country of many gods, one more did not pose much of a challenge.

The Delhi Sultanate and then the Mughals brought hundreds of thousands more Muslims into India and built empires whose hierarchy was crowned by members of the Islamic church.

Starting in the 17th century, the Indian subcontinent fell back into the hands of the Hindus, who considered themselves the true and natural inhabitants of India. These were the Maratha. The fall of the Mughals and the rise of their political subordinates was quite accidental since the Maratha were a class of warrior Hindus who were trained by their Mughal masters for military campaigns. It was thanks to the persistence of Chhatrapati Shivaji that the massively oppressed Hindus of the Indian subcontinent were able to come together and eke out a portion of India for themselves.

Shivaji was a member of the elite Maratha clan, and as such, he enjoyed a relatively privileged life despite his Hindu heritage. Due to his aristocracy, Shivaji was able to muster an army and give Hindus hope for restitution of a land in which Hindus ruled over themselves. Shivaji intended to free the enslaved and oppressed alike and turn them to his own cause. 1645/1646 are significant years because this is when Shivaji captured Torna Fort, the first fort he captured which became the foundation of the Maratha Empire. In 1674, Shivaji was successful in his revolt against the Sultan of Bijapur. He carved out a kingdom with Raigad as his capital and was crowned king of Satara. The Bijapur Sultanate was finally defeated and annexed by the Mughal Empire in 1686. By the time Shivaji died in 1680, he had 100,000 soldiers and nearly 300 hilltop forts protecting the nation he'd founded.

Fighting between the Marathas and the Mughals over the next quarter century resulted in an estimated 3 to 4 million deaths, mostly related to starvation from ruined roads and trading routes interrupted by warfare. Having lost so much in terms of basic resources, human lives, and wasted infrastructure, the Mughal Empire began to fracture at the edges. In the north, the foundations of the Sikh Empire emerged, and in the west, the Maratha Empire grew under the rule of a succession of kings and, eventually, an appointed line of prime ministers, known as the peshwas.

Peshwa Baji Rao I served from 1720 to 1740, and during that time, his administration helped to sack the Mughal city of Delhi. With their capital ransacked and much of their empire occupied by enemy troops, the Mughals finally ceded to their attackers and opted to make a peace treaty. The result was an almost total incapacitation of the Mughals, while the Maratha Empire's new borders stretched entirely from west to east across India.

As the burgeoning empire swelled in size, the peshwas had more and more difficulty administrating the growing population. The prime ministers gave up much of their true power in favor of leaving local governors in charge. Because of this shared governance, the Maratha Empire is referred to by many historians as the Maratha Confederacy after the mid-18th century. It is also a term often used by the British, who had just established their own colonial claim on India via the British East India Company.

Chapter 15 – The British East India Company

The 15th and 16th centuries were known to Europe as the Age of Discovery. Explorers traveled by ship, on horseback, and on foot to find new, distant lands and see what they had to offer. For wealthy nations like England, the world was expanding, and one of the most exciting discoveries was that of exotic, far-away India. Decorated with sparkling jewels and full of aromatic, exotic spices that tickled and delighted the taste buds, India was right where commercial traders from the West wanted to be. It was so popular, in fact, that Christopher Columbus accidentally discovered the New World in his haste to find a shortcut. For the English, a nation whose middle class was growing and able to indulge just a little bit more than it had been in previous centuries, cultivating a lasting relationship with India seemed the logical thing to do.

India and Great Britain were connected by trade as early as the 16th century, during the rule of England's Queen Elizabeth I. British merchants sailed east in search of Indian and Chinese ports after the Portuguese settlements had been in place for years, but their journeys did not go unrewarded. Just as Portugal, China, Afghanistan, and many others had found veritable fortunes in the form of merchant and factory agreements with India, so too did England stake a claim that would change the futures of both countries.

It was especially pertinent for England during that time to expand its empire, since Spain and Portugal were busy splitting up the New World for themselves. In Europe, England was a small but respectable kingdom; as neighboring European nations created worldwide empires, however, England could have easily been swallowed up by those very same colonial forces. To establish herself among the most important and wealthiest of her peers, Queen Elizabeth I looked not primarily to the west but to the east. Whereas the Americas clearly had an immense store of gold that was now flowing into Spain, India had a variety of functional resources that included silk, cotton, fabric dyes, salt, tea, gunpowder, and opium.

On December 31st, 1600, the queen granted a royal charter to the newly founded East India Company (EIC), giving it the funds and internal structure she personally believed would benefit her kingdom the most. To facilitate business between the two countries and halt the skirmishes between the EIC and other trade companies, King James I (Elizabeth's successor in 1603) made an agreement with the Mughal Emperor Jahangir to obtain some of its lands in exchange for access to valuable trade items from Europe.

England and Portugal were not the only European nations from which travelers and traders came to India. In the early 17th century, Dutch, French, and Danish merchants established their own trade routes between home and India and set up their own depots and factories. With so many commercially minded Europeans coming onto the scene, Indian producers quickly realized that they could start charging more for in-demand supplies like silk, cotton, cinnamon, and cardamom. When the prices went up, the British knew the only way to knock costs back down was to get rid of the competition.

Though British occupation in India was at first intended solely for commercial purposes, the company was almost immediately militarized against the other foreign trading communities in the area. Soldiers regularly fought against the encroaching forces of their Dutch and Portuguese rivals while also using the sword to gain control over more land. In true European fashion, the separate entities started fortifying their trading posts with stone walls. The infighting came to a breaking point just a few decades later when local administrators and rulers also became involved in the skirmishes. Such behavior characterized most of the 17th century.

A century later, these nations had inextricably embedded themselves in the Indian landscape, capitalizing on the slow downfall of the Mughal Empire. With the local regimes crumbling, British soldiers were dispatched to India to defend their commercial lands against various armies vying for control of the subcontinent. Successful in its bid to maintain Indian territory, the company itself made the quite unprecedented decision to fight for even more land. Also using the opportunity of political unrest to their gain, the Netherlands, Portugal, France, and Denmark fought for their own territory.

In an attempt to settle things amicably with the powers that be, in 1698, the EIC bribed Mughal officials for zamindari rights over three villages in Bengal—that is, the same type of rights held by aristocrats and lords over their appointed tracts of land. Practicing careful diplomacy, they were even granted a farman (similar to a royal charter) from Emperor Aurangzeb. Those villages were called Sutanuti, Gobindapur, and Kalikata; they eventually grew into the modern city of Kolkata, formerly known as Calcutta.

The farman granted by the emperor was economically disadvantageous for Indians in that it required no taxation on any items bought locally to sell in European markets. Bengal stood to lose millions of pounds of income while the British company gathered immense wealth. In addition to the formal business being conducted throughout Britain's numerous on-site factories and trading posts, many members of the East India Company were making illegal transactions outside the jurisdiction of the company. By the early part of the 18th century, Bengal's representatives had had enough.

When Emperor Aurangzeb died in 1707, the Mughal Empire lost a great deal of its influence and power over the nation. Regional rulers known as nawabs preferred to journey home and administrate locally. The same was true for Bengal's nawab, Murshid Quli Khan. He returned to Bengal with a great feat ahead of him: controlling the unwieldy operations of the East India Company. Khan tried frantically to bring the British traders to heel, but they were firmly implanted on the landscape and equipped with masses of their own soldiers. Khan was relegated to liaison between his native people and the company, as were his successors.

By 1857, the Mughal Empire had come to an end with the death of the last emperor, Bahadur Shah II, and the country was thrown into chaos and uncertainty. The empire was broken, British aristocracy had control over most of the country, and there was little the regional leaders could do to fight the powerful British Empire. In Calcutta, the EIC was ordered to stop fortification efforts around their city by the Nawab of Bengal, Siraj ud-Daulah—and his instructions were ignored. The company was finished with diplomacy.

Chapter 16 – East India Company Rule

Facing constant pressure from other European merchant companies in India, the British focused their energy on strengthening the city's main military outpost, Fort William. Outraged that his order to stop such fortifications had gone unheeded, Siraj ud-Daulah marched on Calcutta with 50,000 soldiers, 500 elephants, and 50 cannons in June of 1756. Unprepared for such an attack, the British troops fled Fort William for the relative safety of their ships in the nearby harbor. Ud-Daulah's forces easily entered the city and took everyone prisoner.

There was one prison room within the walls of the city, and it measured about 20 square meters (215 square feet). Though plenty of space for a few petty criminals, it was not at all equipped to hold the 164 prisoners of war who the Nawab imprisoned there. Most within the cell, known henceforth as the Black Hole of Calcutta, either suffocated or were trampled to death. When the Nawab ordered the door open the next morning at 6 a.m., only a reported 21 people had survived.

News spread quickly to Lieutenant Colonel Robert Clive, stationed with British troops at Fort Saint George in Madras. When repeated attempts at diplomacy met with no answer, Clive made haste for Fort William with Admiral Charles Watson, a contingent of soldiers, and their Indian allies. Clive's forces liberated the British and Indian prisoners of the Nawab on January 2nd, 1757, and took their own prisoners. With Fort William secure, Clive marched onward in search of the nawab himself, who had moved on from Calcutta before British reinforcement had arrived.

Continued attacks by Clive on ud-Daulah's army convinced the latter to attempt the diplomacy he had not bothered with after the siege of Fort William, but it was too late to talk. Hounded by the British wherever he went, Nawab Siraj ud-Daulah staged one last violent stand against the commercial colonialists. Members of the French East India Company were more than willing to help, especially since France was currently at war with Great Britain. It was a fight that Monsieur Sinfray, a French artillery officer, was willing to join.

Siraj ud-Daulah mustered a huge army of more than 60,000 soldiers with the help of fellow Mughal leaders and Sinfray. On the opposing side were a mere 3,000, pieced together from British soldiers and European or Indian allies, all under the leadership of Robert Clive. Each side was well-armed with guns, swords, and cannons, and despite being extremely outnumbered, Clive was feeling bolstered by his recent retaking of the city of Calcutta. On June 23rd, 1757, these forces met at Palashi, West Bengal, about 150 kilometers (93 miles) from the EIC's base.

Outwardly, it seemed pure folly to enter into battle in such conditions, but Robert Clive had a secret: he'd bribed a member of Siraj ud-Daulah's party—Mir Jafar—to defect in exchange for political power under British rule in the area. Clive was confident in his plans, yet when the battle began that morning at Palashi, there was no sign that Jafar would be sending any assistance his way. Instead, Jafar's regiment appeared on the battlefield with orders to hold back until they were given a signal, either to back the British or the Indians.

Nevertheless, Clive and his 3,000 men fought their attackers for several hours, cleverly holding off the advance without losing a great number of soldiers. Around midday, heavy rains set in, soaking the gunpowder stores on the Mughal and French side. Clive's troops wrestled with tarps to protect their own stores and subsequently gained substantially on their enemies in the following gun battle. One of Siraj's most important men, Mir Madan Khan, was killed by cannon fire, leaving the Mughal leader extremely distraught.

Seeing Siraj so close to retreat, Mir Jafar sent word to Clive to push onward. Soon afterward, ud-Daulah left the battlefield altogether, never having set foot in the fray. He took 2,000 troops with him but did not call his remaining soldiers back from the entanglement. Jafar's own regiment of several thousand troops remained, and eventually, there were none left but his and Clive's soldiers. Clive occupied the nawab's empty military camp by five o'clock that evening, and the battle was finished.

Robert Clive and his allies had not just banished Siraj ud-Daulah from their cities; they had effectively changed the political fabric of the province. As promised, Mir Jafar was appointed the new nawab of Bengal, answerable to the administration of the East India Company. Starting in the year 1758, Company Rule was established throughout a massive chunk of eastern India. It was also called Company Raj, "raj" being the Hindu word for rule. Company Rule would persist for one hundred years.

Chapter 17 – The British Raj

"Praise to our Indian brothers, and the dark face have his due!

Thanks to the kindly dark faces who fought with us, faithful and few,

Fought with the bravest among us, and drove them, and smote them, and slew.

That ever upon the topment roof our banner in India blew."

(Alfred Tennyson)

Fort St. George became Madras, and later Chennai, and it was here the British centered their colonial rule over India. British soldiers had already been imported to help the trading company deal with competition from other European traders, so all that was left was to keep expanding westward until the East India Company had authority over a wide ribbon of land that stretched from the southernmost point of India to the easternmost point at Plassey, then back west along the northern border. By the mid-19th century, Britain was effectively in control of the majority of the subcontinent. The original royal charter that funded the continued Company Rule over Indian lands had expired, however, and was only guaranteed 20 years extension at a time.

The British Crown and its government had been imposing more and more on the sovereignty of the East India Company with each renewed contract, and when the locals revolted in 1857, Queen Victoria had the charter canceled altogether. In Parliament, the Government of India Act of 1858 was passed, which stipulated that the EIC be liquidated and all its assets and lands handed over to the British Crown.

The rebellion had begun in May of 1857 when Indian members of the Company Army mutinied in several cities. At odds with their colonial superiors over land taxes, social reforms, and racial discrimination, the sepoys—as these soldiers were called—incited a violent rebellion in which they broke from the EIC and tried to declare themselves a sovereign nation within the company's lands. To this end, rebels met with the last ruler of the Mughals, Bahadur Shah Zafar, and named him as their emperor. They captured large sections in the northwest and held many of the cities there for nearly two years before the EIC regained control through violent, sometimes cruel, warfare.

It was the first day of November 1858 when Queen Victoria issued a direct proclamation to Indians explaining that Company Rule was over. She promised to provide her Indian subjects with similar rights as British subjects. For the great many Indians and sepoys who had fought on the side of the Company and their British colleagues during the rebellion, the words and promises of the British queen were a great comfort. The British Raj began thenceforth, with faith and confidence on both sides. The 82-year-old Emperor Bahadur Shah Zafar was convicted of conspiracy and deported to Rangoon, in British-controlled Burma.

As the British government took control, Victoria gave the existing kingdoms and principalities of India the option of joining her union. The realms that did so were referred to as Princely States, and they kept their own king or ruler as a figurehead and liaison between the state and the British government. Realms who did not wish to join eventually did so by force, losing their independence altogether. These were called the Provinces. Provinces were ruled directly by British administrators. In effect, Great Britain ended up with all of India under its authority, though about 40 percent of that territory was comprised of Princely States. These included Rajasthan, Hyderabad, Jammu and Kashmir, Mysore, and the Baluchistan states.

Within the first four years of official British rule over the vast majority of the subcontinent, the foreign administration not only enacted the Indian Councils Act but dealt with a famine in the Doab region. The former established a working administration in which there were several main departments: revenue, military, law, and finance. The second event was not so simple, and between 1860 and 1861, an estimated two million people starved to death. News of the horrid conditions and unprecedented deaths spread internationally. The following excerpt came from *The New York Times* on March 30, 1861:

> From 400 to 500 deaths a day seems a too moderate computation. Under the brazen sky, young and old, the feeble and the strong, lie down on the iron ground and die. The streets of Delhi are packed with gaunt, despairing wretches, whom a handful of rice would reprieve. Women and children, too weak to eat the food that pity puts into their mouths, expire in the effort to swallow it. Mothers in Travancore sell their pretty children for sixpence, or a bowl of rice, to low-caste buyers -- and die when that is gone. -- Men in Cutch graze and browse, like cattle.

India recovered, though famine had come many times before and it would come again. In the years following the tragedy, Britain took on a variety of important projects in order to strengthen and sustain the newest part of its empire. Railroads were constructed, trade operations were managed better than before, and a world-changing agricultural operation was employed in Darjeeling. Tea was about to revolutionize Indian farming and exports.

Tea had been one of the most popular imports from Asia for centuries by that point, but it came largely from China, and the powerful Qing Dynasty forbade the export of its tea seeds and plants. Scottish botanist, Robert Fortune, was tasked with infiltrating the Chinese tea industry, learning how to process the goods and getting some of the raw materials back home. Fortune dressed as a wealthy Mandarin and took a local companion with him to act as his servant. The servant told the factory administrators that his master had traveled a great distance to see how such wonderful tea was made, and he was politely admitted within.

Fortune managed to learn everything he needed to know and smuggle the important specimens out of China in specially constructed glass cases. In all, he shipped an estimated 20,000 tea plants to England this way. He also smuggled several varieties of roses and other plants that captured his interest. The tea and the flowers proved best suited for India, rather than the British Isles. They were transplanted into fields in Darjeeling and tended by Chinese workers who had also been illegally exported from China. Though the plants had a rough start and many didn't survive, India soon overtook China as the world's largest tea producer.

With agriculture, industry, and infrastructure evolving, Britain concentrated on educating and "civilizing" the Indians under their command. It was made mandatory for schools to teach in English, though most schools were comprised only of male students. To know English was to be better prepared for administrative and well-paid jobs under the Raj, and therefore the gender gap in education kept most females from earning decent wages, if not totally from any sort of gainful employment. In addition to mandating the use of English and Anglican church service attendance, the British Crown encouraged its Indian subjects to mimic English culture in terms of sports and fashion.

Despite all the effort spent on transforming Indians into British subjects, India was called "The Jewel in the Crown of the British Empire." It provided Great Britain with all the tea it could drink plus extra to sell to continental Europe. All the goods exported to the British Isles from India in 1910 were valued at 137,000 British pounds, but that wasn't all India had to give. The Indian Army made up a significant portion of Britain's military resources, which were in heavy use across the empire and during WWI and WWII. Before the first quarter of the 20th century passed, however, India had become restless under British rule. The middle class had grown under the influence of Great Britain, and now it yearned for self-rule.

Chapter 18 – The Caste System

"My method is atheism. I find the atheistic outlook provides a favorable background for cosmopolitan practices. Acceptance of atheism at once pulls down caste and religious barriers between man and man. There is no longer a Hindu, a Muslim or a Christian. All are human beings."

(Gora, *An Atheist with Gandhi*)

As India underwent political, economic, and religious changes over the millennia, an invisible hierarchy was established that persisted despite foreign rule, internal warfare, agricultural and pastoral developments, and the establishment of Buddhism: it was the caste system. Like the formal and informal class divisions of modern societies—lower-class, middle-class, upper-class—castes defined economic realities for India's people, though it was initially more definitive of the roles each person played within the community. According to Hindu literature, the caste system divides Hindus into groups based on their work and their duty, or karma and dharma. These groups contain Brahmins, Kshatriyas, Vaishyas, and Shudras.

Hindus believe that these caste groupings came from Brahma himself, the God of creation, and therefore each of the groups is based on a body part of Brahma. The most valuable and therefore the most influential people were Brahmans, who came from Brahma's head. These are intellectuals and teachers. Beneath these are the Kshatriyas, from Brahma's arms. They are the warriors and kings. Next are the Vaishyas, from Brahma's thighs, responsible for trade. From Brahma's feet came the Shudras, responsible for manual labor. The Dalits, or untouchables, were on the lowest rung of the hierarchical ladder; they were left the job of cleaning toilets and sweeping streets. Technically speaking, the Dalits aren't even in the caste system but exist outside of it.

Though it's easy to imagine such a system being economically viable in the prehistorical days when India's villages and towns only had so many roles to fill, these divisions were actually quite psychologically influential. The castes lived apart in separate sections of the community, each avoiding the other's wells and public spaces. People married only within their caste and did not eat or drink with members of the others. When Muslim conquerors entered India, the caste system stayed firmly in place, with the exception of those Hindus who converted to Islam.

In addition to the original four castes, 25,000 more sub-castes were created to specifically address each niche role with the community. Theoretically, if a person born into the Shudra caste, whose family's job is making bricks, then Shudra brick-making is the destiny of all that person's children, grandchildren, great-grandchildren, and so on. Technically speaking, Hinduism does leave room for passion to play a role in optional sub-castes; though, the reality is, by and large, that where one is born, one remains. Though there are rare exceptions to the rule, castes effectively oppressed the poor and kept the wealthy just as influential as were their ancestors. Personal ambition meant very little unless you were Brahman.

When the Maratha Hindus reclaimed much of the subcontinent for their own purposes, the castes were reinforced with vigor as Hindus had been waiting for an opportunity to fully practice their religion and lifestyle for centuries. Castes weren't just a traditional part of societal organization; they could actually be interpreted as the will of the universe for a culture that believed in reincarnation. Hindu texts teach their followers that the soul exists despite the death of the body and that one's soul can be reborn in new bodies again and again, either in hell, in heaven, or on earth. Through successive earthly incarnations, the soul is born into a caste according to its karma (in this case used to mean "the total sum of one's actions") and therefore has the chance to become a better person in each new life. Theoretically, one's soul might first live on earth as a Dalit and through good deeds achieve the Shudra label in its next life until finally reaching the top of the hierarchy and ultimately become "moksha," the final spiritual level at which point no more lives are necessary. At moksha, one reaches purity and immortality.

On a spiritual level, these are admirable concepts. In practice, they imposed a highly unfair burden on members of the lower castes or those branded untouchables. Much like the lower, middle, and upper class divides of other societies, those at the bottom are much more plentiful than those at the top. The system established itself just as economy demanded; more than 90 percent of Indians have traditionally belonged to the untouchable group or the Shudra level, where they worked long hours in agriculture, manufacturing, or garbage and waste management. Meanwhile, precious few enjoyed the benefits of birth into the Brahmin group, in whose embrace they could expect to find administrative jobs with shorter hours and higher pay.

Within families, inter-caste marriages were very much frowned upon, as higher castes took a great deal of pride in their station. When castes did mix, dining etiquette—from table arrangements to the type of food served—became quite tricky. For as many ways as there are to divide a population based on economic and ancestral status, each of them seems to have manifested itself in the practice of cooking, sharing, and eating food. The different types of food preparation are themselves judged as either "pukka" (perfect) or "kacca" (undressed), and only the former type is appropriate to share with others.

Specifically, kacca foods are simply boiled, steamed, or stewed dishes; served without any type of fat, they are acceptable as part of family meals or to give to servants. Pukka foods have been deep-fried in clarified butter, or "ghee," which means they are protected from outside impurities, according to Hindu tradition. The historical writer Margaret Visser says, "When a Brahmin gives a feast and wants as many people as possible to come, he chooses a menu of *pukka* food and cooks it himself, for his touch can pollute nobody."

Though castes are not outwardly obvious in terms of skin color or clothing, many Indian surnames denote the hierarchy of his or her family. It is one of the few oppressive regimes in the world in which the people who are revered and the people who are impoverished are genetically one and the same.

Chapter 19 – Mohandas Gandhi

"If this Empire seems an evil thing to me, it is not because I hate the British, I hate only the Empire."

(Gandhi)

India needed a homegrown hero, and it found one by the name of Mohandas Karamchand Gandhi—better known as "Mahatma" Gandhi, or "high-souled" in Sanskrit. Born to a family within the sub-caste of Baniya on October 2nd, 1869, Gandhi spent his early childhood in the coastal princely state of Porbandar. True to his high caste, his father, Karamchand, had an administrative position as the chief minister of Porbander State. Karamchand married four times; his first two wives died, and he had a polygamous marriage with the second two. His fourth wife, Putlibai, had four children, the last of whom would help lead India out of the colonial age and into a new era of republicanism.

Gandhi's father was an average Hindu, but his mother worshiped a subsect of Hinduism, known as Pranami Vaishnavism. Putlibai's religion focused on Lord Vishnu, who is considered by members of her sect to be the supreme lord of all other deities, including Lord

Krishna, who is considered another embodiment of Vishnu. Gandhi's mother was a very devout woman, who regularly performed fasts she believed purified her body and mind. Her influence would have a great effect on Mohandas when he became a politically minded adult.

The family moved to Rajkot in 1874, and there, Mohandas and his siblings attended school. As was custom, boys were married to a girl his parents chose for him. At the time of the wedding, Mohandas was 13 years old, and his bride, Kasturbai Makhanji Kapadia, was fourteen. Still in their teens, the young couple welcomed their first baby in 1885, but it died in infancy, sadly within months of Mohandas' own father. The loss weighed heavily on Gandhi, who was still attending high school. A few years later, he graduated and immediately looked to enroll for post-secondary studies in the cheapest college of his state. Soon after being accepted, however, he dropped out and decided to pursue legal studies in Great Britain.

Mohandas' brother, already a British-trained lawyer, supported this decision and offered to help with expenses. Putlibai, however, was worried that her son would be tempted to cast aside his Hindu beliefs if he spent so much time away from India. Even the local chief told 18-year-old Gandhi that if he left home, he would be banished from his caste. Unconcerned, Mohandas made the journey to London and accepted his enrollment at London's University College.

The young student had promised his family that he would continue to abstain from alcohol, meat, and extramarital affairs, and this was a promise he took seriously. Unfortunately, he found very little to eat in London that suited his vegetarian diet. Eventually, he found a lonely vegetarian restaurant in the city and befriended many of its patrons, who elected him an executive member of the Vegetarian Society. It was this society that turned Mohandas' social life around, as he met many Hindus, Buddhists, and theological philosophers with whom he could discuss his own beliefs and hopes for the future.

Having earned his law degree and passed the necessary exams to establish a practice of his own, Gandhi left London at age 22 to discover the devastating news that during his studies, his mother had passed away. After several years of struggling to set up a law office in India, the young man accepted a legal position in the Colony of Natal, South Africa. He set sail in 1893 alone, expecting to work in Natal for about one year.

The blatant racism Gandhi experienced in South Africa, then a British colony, was not only humiliating but politically eye-opening. Mohandas believed himself to be a British citizen equal to those in any other colony, but outside of India, it became clear that white British citizens held themselves above others. Non-whites were denied seats on the bus, expected not to mix with white people, and generally harassed and beaten for a plethora of supposed indiscretions that may or may not have been imagined. Perplexed and disoriented, Mohandas completed the legal project he'd been recruited for and made plans to return to India—he didn't follow through on those plans. Instead, he merely collected his family and headed back to the Colony of Natal, inspired to help the Indians there with much-needed legal reform.

Though at first, Gandhi was singularly focused on the plight of Indians in Natal, he eventually extended that empathy to the oppressed native black people of South Africa. By the time the British Empire declared war on the Zulu Kingdom in 1906, Mohandas had realized that it was not only his own people who had been pressed under the heel of Great Britain. To demonstrate solidarity between Indians and Africans, Gandhi organized a group of stretcher bearers whose self-imposed duty it was to collect and provide care for wounded soldiers from both sides of the fight. In many cases, the group was barricaded from helping the Zulus, and black members of the stretcher bearers were shot by British soldiers.

Disheartened at humanity's natural tendency toward violence and hierarchy, Gandhi moved out to a farm near Johannesburg and founded Tolstoy Farm. Together with his friend, Hermann

Kallenbach, Tolstoy Farm was dedicated to peaceful, communal living and the philosophy of peaceful reform through nonviolence. Mohandas lived at the farm for five years, meditating on his own ideas of ideal politicism and protest, before he was urged to return to India by none other than the leader of the Indian National Congress. He returned, ready to march again with his Indian brothers and sisters in search of independence.

It was Gopal Krishna Gokhale who summoned Gandhi and his family back from South Africa. He took it upon himself to update Gandhi, who was by then revered by international Indian communities as a leader, on the political issues facing India that year, 1915. The Home Rule League was being launched by Annie Besant, and throughout the country, Indians were asking themselves whether there was anything to be gained from remaining a colony of Great Britain. The Independent India movement started to gain traction, especially under the influence of Gandhi.

Before he could succeed in separating India from Great Britain, however, Gandhi had to unite his own people to work together toward the betterment of India. He traveled to Champaran in 1917 to help the local, impoverished farmers as they made demands on the British administration. His diplomacy brought about much-needed changes. The next year in Kheda, following disastrous floods, Mohandas rallied the people to stand firm in their resolve not to pay taxes on money they were unable to earn. The holdout lasted five long months, but Britain eventually gave in. In 1919, the activist began important talks with his country's Muslim leaders, asking that they band together with Hindus and other groups in pushing for relief from colonial rule. That same year, the British government passed the Rowlatt Act, by which any suspected terrorist in British India could be imprisoned for up to two years without a trial. The terrorism of which the government spoke had been on a small scale, but it was committed to responding to the growing anti-colonial movement.

Gandhi and others were highly publicly critical of the Rowlatt Act. They scheduled rallies and demonstrations during which protesters prayed, fasted, and protested peacefully. In some cities, however, the demonstrations turned to rioting, which led Gandhi to order them stopped. He could not support widespread protests unless they were strictly violence free. When the act came into effect, two leading members of the National Congress—Dr. Satya Pal and Dr. Saifuddin Kitchlew—were arrested. To prevent further protests, the army was sent into Punjab during the same week as many Sikhs traveled there to celebrate Baisakhi Day. On April 13th, peaceful protests in Amritsar against the deportation of more political leaders sparked a response from the army and fighting soon got out of control. More than hundreds of people were murdered and over a thousand were injured at the hands of the army. Thereafter, it was called the Massacre of Amritsar.

With the army operating under the leadership of the British Crown, the Baisakhi Day killings convinced most Indians that Great Britain was indeed the enemy. Angry that his compatriots could not keep their protesting violence free and avoid the wrath of the British guards, Gandhi began a fast to try to inspire his countrymen and women to consider their actions more carefully. Two years later, Mohandas himself was put in charge of the Indian National Congress, and there was no question in which direction he wanted to take his political party.

Muslim outreach went well when Gandhi expressed his support of the Turkish Caliphate, but it disappeared just as quickly when that Turkish regime collapsed in 1922. Even so, he had a great deal of the country's popular support. People called him "Mahatma" and followed his example of non-cooperation with British legislation. They boycotted British goods and tried to only buy Indian products. Gandhi himself wore only plain garments spun from Indian wool, denouncing expensive clothing items that not all of his fellow Indians could afford to wear.

Gandhi was arrested on March 10th, 1922, for sedition. Sentenced to six years in prison, he only served two before being released for medical reasons. Following an appendicitis operation, the political leader was released and quickly returned to his work.

Chapter 20 – The Salt March and Independence

"Peace is not a relationship of nations. It is a condition of mind brought about by a serenity of soul. Peace is not merely the absence of war. It is also a state of mind. Lasting peace can come only to peaceful people."

(Jawaharlal Nehru)

While Mohandas Gandhi worked to cultivate a peaceful revolution, his compatriot, Jawaharlal Nehru, followed a similar path. Born in 1889 in Ahallabad, British India, Nehru went to Trinity College, Cambridge, and earned a degree in natural science. Following graduation, he moved to London and studied law at Inner Temple before returning to India to become a practicing lawyer.

It wasn't until Indians under British rule started protesting openly in the 1910s that Nehru joined politics—and it all started with his attendance of the annual Indian National Congress in 1912. A political party comprised mostly of moderates, Congress seemed disturbingly elite to Nehru. He immediately noticed that its members were all English speaking, mostly members of wealthy families. Despite misgivings based on these observations, Nehru decided to go ahead and work with the party in pursuit of Indian civil rights.

In 1930, Nehru joined tens of thousands of other Indians in following Gandhi's plan for disruptive civil disobedience against the British government. Mohandas reasoned that the salt tax, which had been in place since 1882 and required all Indians to buy high-priced salt only from the British, offered the perfect opportunity for a mass demonstration. It was illegal to gather salt, so the protestors decided to walk to the coastal town of Dandi on the Arabian Sea and do just that. Dandi was 386 kilometers (240 miles) away from their starting point in Sabermanti.

The journey began with only a few dozen participants on March 12th, but as they moved westward, many more joined them along the way. Gandhi spoke to the people of each community they marched through, urging his fellow Indians to join him in breaking the law to prove to Great Britain that there was strength within India to think for itself and throw off the chains of colonial oppression. The newspapers reported on this progress, at first mocking what they viewed as a trifling issue for the protestors to focus on—and yet, Mohandas knew that if any issue could be embraced by every caste and economic hierarchy of India, it was that of overpriced salt. Every household required salt, and India was perfectly capable of producing its own, affordable stock of the mineral.

It had been over a decade since the violent massacre at Amritsar, and Gandhi believed that he and his fellow protestors were ready to make a big scene with zero violence. He was right. As Nehru, Gandhi, and other members of the Indian National Congress made their way to Dandi, the crowds swelled into the tens of thousands by the time the journey reached its end on April 5th. At the edge of India, where seawater met the land, Gandhi walked into the water to make salt. He found that the natural salt crystals from the surf had already been crushed and pounded into the sand by teams of police, but that didn't dissuade him from his purpose. He reached into the wet sand and found a large, uncrushed piece of salt, plucking it from the sea and thereby defying the salt law. Thousands joined him, both in Dandi and other coastal regions, collecting and harvesting their own salt from the sea. Great numbers of those practicing willful civil disobedience were women, proud and at last enabled to speak up for themselves and their nation.

The British government was not amused. Mohandas Gandhi was arrested and put in jail, but his followers were so inspired by the salt march that they went ahead with a protest at the Dharasana Salt Works on May 21st. The police were ready for the disobedience, and when about 2,500 peaceful activists arrived on the scene, the former struck out with clubs. It was another massacre, this time at the hands of native Indians against their own people at the command of the British. Worse, not one of the protestors raised a hand in violence or even self-defense, perfectly executing their ideal of peaceful protest. The police beat down at least 300 people and killed two.

The *United Press* described a brave and commanding woman at the head of the protest pack:

> Prayers said as white-clad volunteers knelt in the moonlight and an impassioned speech by the poetess-leader, Mrs. Sarojini Naidu, opened the mass attack of 2,500 independence demonstrators today on the Dharasana Salt Works. The poetess, wearing a rough, homespun robe and soft slippers, but no stockings, exhorted her followers to the raid in which 260 of them were injured and which brought about her own arrest.

Jawaharlal Nehru was also arrested at the protest as were some 60,000 other Indians found guilty of various disobediences in the aftermath of the clash. Aside from gaining international support for their plight, India won only a little political sway from the non-cooperation movement. Gandhi was personally allowed to meet with the Viceroy of India, Lord Irwin, after being released from prison in

January of 1931 and afterward was given a place at a London conference concerning Indian administration. He was unable to achieve anything further for his country at that conference, and in disappointment, his Indian National Congress colleagues began searching for other methods by which to achieve independence. Nehru and Gandhi drifted apart.

While Mohandas took up the plight of the untouchables of India, Nehru remained with the Congress and continued pushing for self-rule. Finally, in 1947, they achieved their goal. At midnight on August 15th, the Indian Independence Act came into effect, splitting British India into the Dominions of India and Pakistan. A few years later, these were reasserted as the Republic of India and the Islamic Republic of Pakistan. The Indian National Congress was put in power of the new republic with Jawaharlal Nehru at the head of government as India's first prime minister. India was finally independent.

Chapter 21 – Wildlife, Then and Now

"The greatness of a nation and its moral progress can be judged by
the way its animals are treated."

(Mohandas Gandhi)

Though the initial placement of the Indian National Congress in
power over the new Dominion was temporary, it was officially voted
into that same office following the country's first democratic
election. It was an important step not only toward the better
organization of the country's resources and infrastructure but toward
more complex forms of self-care. There were a great many ways in
which the new India hoped to better itself, and that included finding
ways to care for the physical landscape and the creatures that
dwelled within the Dominion of India.

The flora and fauna of the Indian subcontinent are just as splendid,
diverse, and amazing as the people and the culture. Ten thousand
years ago, massive woolly mammoths roamed the land and began to
evolve into a beloved member of this part of the world: the Indian
elephant. A sub-species of the larger Asian elephant, these elephants
have shared their ancestral home with an array of fascinating
creatures, from the Bengal tiger and the Indian rhinoceros to the

snow leopard and the Indian peafowl. Several millennia spent alongside India's human communities has had perhaps the most lasting influence on these wildlife populations.

We've already discussed the fates of those great elephants who became the pets and favored warriors of India's earliest tribes. Trained from infancy to follow the commands of their human masters, hundreds of thousands of Asian elephants helped shape the political landscape of the ancient subcontinent. They were the pride of the Mauryan Army and the Mughal Army; even the East India Company had 1,500 war elephants in its military armory that were used during the Sepoy Rebellion of 1857. Though the use of war elephants declined in the 20th century, elephants remained useful during the Second World War when British India used them to help transport building materials and manipulate logs for road and bridge building.

After a lifetime of human alliance, a creature whose numbers used to be in the hundreds of thousands for each regional warlord was estimated at fewer than 35,000 in the wild. Modern India's elephants have been hunted for sport, killed out of fear, and suffered dwindling numbers due to loss of natural habitat. They are listed as a formally endangered species by the International Union for Conservation of Nature, but the future isn't necessarily so dark for these precious creatures. In 1992, the Indian government's Ministry of Environment and Forests launched Project Elephant, a strategy to protect elephants and their habitats, confront the issues between human communities and elephants, and look toward the welfare of domesticated elephants.

Elephants aren't the only India animal facing extinction. They are joined by their massive feline cohabitators, the Bengal tigers, on the IUCN endangered species list. Revered for its size, power, and beautiful orange and black-striped coat, the Bengal tiger is sadly down to about 2,500 individuals in the wilds of India, though it is officially the National Animal of India. Tiger numbers have diminished immensely in just the last few centuries, mostly due to big game hunting. Preserved hides of these tigers were prized by many British colonialists who lived in India during the Raj, and the heads of these hunted cats are still considered wonderful trophies for some sports hunters.

Big game hunting by no means began with the British, of course. The industry really became big business in India when the 16th century Mughal Emperor Jalal-ud-din Muhammad Akbar arranged sport hunting safaris for himself and important visiting dignitaries. From that time, the country's aristocrats—be they Mongol, Turkic, Afghan, or otherwise—spent their leisure time on horseback or astride massive elephants, searching for the most dangerous predators of the forests and grasslands to shoot and kill. Tigers were the most passionately hunted.

Also known as the Royal Bengal, these giant cats naturally inhabit the forests, grasslands, and mangroves of India, hunting deer, sambars, nilgais, buffalos, and gaurs at night and sleeping most of the hot day away. They were revered—just as Indian elephants were—in ancient communities of the Indus River Valley. The Pashupati seal of the Indus Valley Civilization bears the likeness of this large-eyed, wide-faced cat, and in Vedic and Hindu mythology, the tiger is symbolic of power. Even the Goddess Durga sat astride a Bengal tiger while she traveled on Earth. Today, there is a very real possibility that the Royal Bengal tiger could be lost altogether, remaining only in artworks and Indian postage stamps.

Prime Minister Indira Gandhi, the first female to govern India since Razia Sultana of the Delhi Sultanate, made a government mandate to save her nation's tigers. In 1973, she enacted Project Tiger as a means to protect the country's newly elected National Animal from extinction and murder at the hands of hunters. Multiple conservation efforts have been put in place to save the tiger, including the establishment of more than 50 tiger preserves, but it has proved very difficult to positively impact the Bengal's population. The Sariska Tiger Reserve in Rajasthan declared that it lost every one of its 16 protected tigers in 2005, a loss due mostly to poaching. In addition to the tiger's coat, the Bengal's teeth and bones are considered vital ingredients for Chinese medicines, which makes the cat exceptionally valuable to poachers. Project Tiger has been a challenge, but as the world's most tiger-rich country, India has managed to increase its wild tiger count by about 30 percent.

The government and people of India have worked hard to move from a culture of big game hunting to species preservationists, particularly with the rare animals who struggle the most to deal with growing human populations. India's over 500 wildlife sanctuaries help the nation care for its wildlife and also boost the country's tourism. Tourists and Indians alike have shown great interest in—and empathy for—the big cats of the subcontinent, who can rarely be seen in other parts of the world. The endangered snow leopards of the Himalayas are just one of the stunning species of big cats to call India home. It's large paws, long fur, and black, gray, and white spotted pattern sets it apart from its larger tiger and lion cousins of the forests. Several of these beautiful panthers can be found in Hemis National Park in Kashmir and Jammu.

Preservation has taken over the whole of India, with nearly every creature finding niche refuge in at least one park or facility. One-horned rhinoceros frolic at the Kaziranga National Park in Assam, Kashmir stags find refuge at Dachigam, and the Asiatic lions proudly guard their prides in Gujarat's Gir Forest National Park. Pre-history and the early Modern Age may have been tough on India's precious animals, but the people are working hard to shelter and care for the species that also call India home.

Chapter 22 – A Brief History of the Curry

> "It is a shame that Mama doesn't use the hundreds of other fruits and vegetables and spices available from around the world. If it isn't Indian, according to her, it isn't good."

(Amulya Malladi, Indian author)

Since the very first steps taken by an outsider into the subcontinent of cardamom, turmeric, ginger, fenugreek, and an astounding assortment of herbs, aromatics, and natural preservatives, it was clear that India had something very special simmering in the kitchen. Much generalization has been made of these diverse and succulent dishes even since the days of trading along the Silk Road, but simply speaking, there is a collection of long-beloved ingredients used by most Indian cooks, whether they live in New Delhi or Chennai. These come together in a hundred different ways to create what we've come to describe as a "curry": a heavily spiced dish cooked in the Indian style.

The famous curries of India are not without their own set of dining rules. Typically, Indians sit on the floor with their legs crossed to partake of a meal. It is a tradition that likely has its roots in the Vedic way of life since the posture mimics that of Sukhasan, an important Yogic pose. Instead of the high tables and chairs predominant in most Western dining rooms, the classical Indian dining area features a low table surrounded by several cushions. Diners use their hands and pieces of flatbread to eat.

There is a traditional collection of dining habits and manners that are expected to be used at the Indian table. It is considered customary at a formal table to sit down with freshly washed hands and keep the serving utensils from mixing in the dishes—the latter rule out of respect for the vegetarians among the diners. Washing your hands is not just important for one diner but for everyone at the table since it is customary to eat with one's right hand. Passing food with the left hand helps to keep the dining area free of cross-contamination.

From the early Indus River Valley days, household living areas featured meals cooked from the bountiful crops of the floodplains. Harappan farmers grew dependent on a variety of grains that would remain the staple foods for most of India into the modern age. These included wheat, millet, rice, and lentils. Paired with a wide variety of vegetables and spices, these fundamental ingredients were used again and again until cooks learned how to best manipulate them in terms of longevity, flavor, and nutritional satisfaction. Ground whole wheat turned into flat, unleavened breads; lentils could be ground into flour, boiled into soups, or spiced to stand alone as a main dish. As the Harappan people spread along the Indus Valley and southward along the Sarasvati, they learned to mix a colorful collection of vegetables and fruits into their stews, including eggplant, onion, taro, mango, and tamarind.

Archaeological research into the utensils and dental remains of the Harappans of ancient Farmana, situated in northern Haryana, revealed that recipes of the ancient Indians were not at all dissimilar than are in use today. Calling it a "proto-curry" of the Harappans, food writer Soiti Bannerjee extrapolated those finds into a simple recipe that would have been prepared in an earthenware pot.

Proto-Curry, circa 2000 BCE

6-7 small aubergines, washed and slit

1-inch piece of ginger, ground

1 fresh turmeric, ground, or ¼ tsp turmeric powder

Salt

1 tbsp. raw mango cut into cubes

2-3 tbsp. sesame oil

¼ tsp. cumin

Dehydrated sugarcane juice to taste

A few leaves of sweet basil (optional)

Many of the Harappans were vegetarians, probably due to the lack of domesticated animals and the plentitude of protein-rich crops in the Indus River Valley. It's also possible that the meatless Vedic religion made its appearance during this period, before the high number of Asian migrants. Around the time of the proto-curry, the necessity to eat only plant-based foods started to change. According to collections of bones found in archaeological sites, it seems that the domesticated chicken may have started its evolutionary journey right along the floodplains of the Indus. Researchers have posited that two species of wild birds, a red junglefowl and a grey junglefowl, interbred to create a type of bird that could not fly well and that was naturally inclined to domestication.

About five centuries later, large groups of Aryans moved onto the subcontinent, bringing with them herds of domesticated cattle that were used only for milk. According to the beliefs of these pastoral people, cows were a sacred and greatly respected part of daily life, and as such, they were not slaughtered for meat. This idea has persisted in many sects of Hinduism and even inspired vegetarianism in as many as 30 percent of today's Indians—with the help of Buddhism and Jainism. So many early people believed fervently in the good of vegetarianism that about 5,000 years ago the notion of a meatless diet was philosophized as a fundamental part of Jainism. Today, it is mandatory for restaurants in India to mark their dishes with a green or red circle, the former indicating that only vegetarian items were used in its preparation.

Though the Aryans did not harm their cows, they were by no means a vegetarian people. They showed the Harappans how to care for domesticated animals such as goats, which quickly became as popular as chickens for a large portion of ancient carnivorous Indians. Though an unusual ingredient for many Westerners, goat remains prominently on menus throughout modern India. Meat and milk aren't the only important pieces of the puzzle introduced to the delectable Indian culinary palette by central Asia, however; the Aryans also brought along mustard, black pepper, and turmeric.

Due to a constant influx of trade, culture, and people in the northern regions of India, it is here we generally see most central and east Asian influences on the regional cooking. Greek and Chinese conquerors had no such beliefs that stopped them from taking animal lives for consumption and their cooking methods involved a hearty mix of rice, chicken, and citrus fruits. Northern India became a culinary hub known for the use of saffron, rich and creamy korma sauces, cheese, milk, roasted chicken, pork, goat, and the soft, puffy white naan breads of the Afghans. Long before the infamous plantations of Indian tea were so much as cultivated, Indians were enjoying tea shipped from China.

Of course, there were yet more ingredients to discover and develop within local cultures. India has a coastline of 7,517 km (4,671 miles) which makes fishing a logical part of the lives of millions who live within reach of the Arabian Sea, the Bay of Bengal, the Laccadive Sea, and the Andaman Sea. Along these immense coastlines, Indians fished, used local ingredients to accompany their fruits of the sea, and created rich culinary traditions. Though not all Hindus agreed with consuming fish, many subsections of the lifestyle welcomed the use of seafood.

Konkan is a coastline along western India that stretches for 720 kilometers (nearly 450 miles) across the modern Indian states of Maharashtra, Goa, and Karnataka. Here, the Malvani people have subsisted on fish curries and rice for hundreds of years. Important dishes along the Konkan include fluffy, fried wheat and millet bread, coconut soup, mutton and chicken curries, fried duck, spicy cashews, and an assortment of seafood. Here, it is common to be served fried mackerel, curried pomfret fish, and curried or fried prawns. Coconut features heavily throughout local recipes, as does the plentiful mango of the region. The large city of Mumbai, historically a part of the Konkan though now politically separate, is home to a range of coastal delicacies that delight the senses.

Also known as Bombay, Mumbai has been packed with various flavors, fish, migrant foods, and street vendors for as long as its inhabitants have been hungry. Where once there was fresh fish, now there are complex vegetarian dishes comprised of chickpea-flour noodles, boiled potatoes, fresh tomato, cilantro (Bombay bhelpuri), exceedingly buttery breads, Persian brun maska, chai tea, and even delicacies like idli dumplings, traditionally found only in the south. There is perhaps no better place to experience the mixture of cultures, religions, and regional ingredients of ancient and modern coast India than here in one of its oldest cities.

South India is famous for a culinary tradition that includes some of the hottest, spiciest dishes in the country, though the chili pepper only arrived on the subcontinent in the mid-16th century. Indigenous to Mesoamerica, these spicy and flavorful little jewels probably came to the southwest coast of India first in the ships of Portuguese traders. In addition to a range of hot and milder curries, southern cuisine features a delicious collection of side dishes, including papadams (large, chickpea-flour crackers), crepe-like dosa breads, fried rice, and fermented lentil cakes (idlis). It is here that you will find a marked difference in the textures of each curry, as most are split between dry presentation (poriyals, served with rice) and watery stews called sambars, rasams, and kootus. Tamarind is a regular ingredient in many of these south Indian recipes, lending a sour and fruity flavor to vegetable and meat plates.

The northern state of Rajasthan is home to India's highest population of vegetarians, who make up nearly 75 percent of the state's citizens—that's over 50 million of almost 69 million people. Neighboring states Haryana and Punjab also have very high percentages of vegetarians, which corresponds with its high rate of Hindus and Jains. West Bengal, Andhra Pradesh, Telangana, and Tamil Nadu are home to most of the nation's meat-eating citizens, with as many as 98 percent of people reportedly consuming meat as a regular part of their diet. In these states, a non-vegetarian form of Hinduism is most prominent. As it always has, India's belief systems have a fundamental impact on its dietary norms. With the movement of even more religious groups into ancient and medieval India, still more ingredients, culinary fusion, and dietary standards were set.

Chapter 23 – The Space Program

"India is not, as people keep calling it, an underdeveloped country,
but rather, in the context of its history and cultural heritage, a highly
developed one in an advanced state of decay."
(Shashi Tharoor)

Prime Minister Jawaharlal Nehru established the India National
Committee for Space Research in 1962 to bring his country into the
space age alongside the Soviet Union and the United States. Though
India did not have the financial resources necessary to race its
colleagues in putting humans on the moon, it did have an
inspirational background of scientific and mathematical minds to
rival any in the world. Under the direction of Dr. Vikran Sarabhai,
the department and its successor, the Indian Space Research
Organization, launched a successful project to manufacture and
launch a satellite into orbit. That satellite, called Aryabhata in honor
of the 6th-century mathematician, did indeed reach orbit in 1975,
thanks to a ride on a Soviet Union rocket. Sarabhai and his
associates also built the Thumba Equatorial Rocket Launching
Station near the southernmost tip of mainland India, very near to
Earth's natural magnetic equator to best facilitate atmospheric
research.

ISRO, the Indian Space Research Organization, replaced Nehru's original agency in 1969. Tasked with developing space-age technology for use within India, as well as cooperating in space exploration, ISRO successfully built an astonishing number of crafts and machinery that aided all space age nations in their pursuit of knowledge. In the first decades of ISRO, the organization mostly focused on building and launching rockets that could bring payloads into orbit around the earth and the moon.

In the 1980s, ISRO made nine successful satellite launches that would be used as broadcasting and communication links. In 1984, the first Indian was sent into space: Rakesh Sharma. Sharma was an Indian Air Force pilot chosen by the Soviet Interkosmos program to fly in the Soyuz T-11 spacecraft to link with the Salyut 7 space station. The mission was a success, and with Rakesh Sharma aboard the Soviet space station as a Research Cosmonaut, his mission was to observe Earth from space. In addition to specific observation schemes, Sharma conducted various experiments that involved bio-medicine, material processing, and remote sensing. In all, Sharma and his Soviet colleagues spent 7 days, 21 hours, and 40 minutes aboard the Salyut 7. This mission made India the 14th nation to send a human into space.

By 1993, India had launched 16 satellites from at least 5 different countries, helping to develop the digital technology of the entire globe. India's communications and space flight specialists continued to launch satellites, building upon their existing knowledge to the point that in 2008, their own lunar orbiter, Chandryaan, was set in place around the moon. Chandrayaan functioned for almost a year and launched its own Moon Impact Probe.

During Chandryaan's 312 days in service, it mapped the chemical characteristics of the moon's surface, using 3D topography. Five Indian-made instruments aided the research, plus six from other participating countries. The points of interest on the lunar surface were its polar regions, as it was hoped that these areas might be hiding water in the form of ice. Indeed, it surveyed the lunar surface to produce a complete map of its chemical characteristics and a 3-dimensional topography chart. Indeed, Chandrayaan became the first lunar mission to find proof of the existence of ice on the moon.

To celebrate the massive achievement of the Indian-led project, the Chandrayaan team received multiple international awards, including the SPACE 2009 Award from the American Institute of Aeronautics and Astronautics, the International Cooperation Award from the International Lunar Exploration Working Group, and the Space Pioneer Award from the National Space Society. The existence of ice on the moon was sensational news for those involved in space exploration because water—in any form—is considered the most important ingredient in the development and evolution of life.

The scientific community went crazy for ISRO's lunar data, but India's space program was far from finished. Another trained Indian astronaut, a woman named Kalpana Chawla, was chosen as part of the six-person crew of the Space Shuttle *Columbia* flight STS-87. The *Columbia* launched on November 19th, 1997, with Chawla on board, in charge of deploying the Spartan satellite.

In 2000, Chawla was selected again to join a new crew for a mission aboard the same space shuttle, but the trip was postponed until 2003. Chawla eventually left Earth again on January 16th, 2003, aboard the *Columbia* with six other astronauts. The launch was successful except that a piece of the shuttle's foam insulation broke apart from the body of the ship and hit the left wing of the spacecraft. The crew spent its time in space conducting natural experiments and documenting the effects of space travel on the human body. Their return to Earth was just a few weeks later, on February 1st, but due to its previous damage, the shuttle became unstable during its reentry into the atmosphere and broke apart. Chawla and her fellow crew members were killed, leading to the grounding of the space shuttle program for several years afterward. Just days after the accident, India's prime minister, Atal Bihari Vajpayee, renamed the space program's meteorological series of satellites "Kalpana-1."

In the years following the *Columbia* disaster, manned-space missions were put on hold, but ISRO was far from idle. Intensive research went into satellite technology, rockets, capsule recovery, troubleshooting, and much, much more. In 2013, India sent an orbiter to Mars, an important step that put their program on par with similar departments of America's National Aeronautics and Space Administration. Not only had ISRO run the same successful mission as NASA, but they'd done it for ten times less money. In an industry where projects always carry a hefty price tag, the ability to put together high-quality, low-cost equipment is truly revolutionary.

The wins kept on coming in the 2010s for India's space program. In 2016, ISRO sent 28 satellites into orbit from Indonesia, Germany, the United States, and Canada. And three years before this, in 2013, they had created their own satellite navigation system—the IRNSS. The Indian Regional Navigation Satellite System was developed to give India's scientists and astronauts primary access to satellite navigation systems instead of relying on the cooperative use of systems run by other nations. The precedent for such technology was set in 1999 when India and Pakistan engaged in armed conflict following the discovery of disguised Pakistani military insurgents crossing the border in Kashmir. The skirmish lasted two months, during which time ISRO was refused access to the American satellite navigation system.

India's space program continues on doggedly, expanding rather than shrinking as many other national space programs did after the initial excitement of the moon landing. By 2022, ISRO hopes to start sending more Indian astronauts into space for exploratory missions involving the moon, Mars, nearby asteroids, and potentially Venus.

Epilogue

"I have lived a long life, and I am proud that I spend the whole of my life in the service of my people. I am only proud of this and nothing else. I shall continue to serve until my last breath, and when I die, I can say, that every drop of my blood will invigorate India and strengthen it."

(Indira Gandhi)

Restructuring India after it won independence from British rule wasn't easy. The divide between India and Pakistan had separated communities with cultural ties and bound others together of opposing faiths. Many people died in successive, minute reorganizations of the border that was meant to keep Muslims in the north and Hindus in the south. Millions of people crossed the border on foot, carrying their belongings and other family members, hoping to live shoulder to shoulder with families of their own faith. There have been ongoing troubles between neighboring regions.

On the whole, today's India is a land of peace, opportunity, and diversity. In the Indian Himalayas, where the ways of the ancient Sarasvati met those of the Tibetans, Nepalese, and Chinese,

Buddhism and simplicity reigns. It is cold and meager among the peaks where families send their oldest boys to the monasteries to learn the teachings of the Dalai Lama. In addition to the sparse religious communities, the mountains and adjacent plateaus are inhabited by a few lingering nomadic tribes. They subsist largely on barley porridge and yak's milk, and in the harsh winter months share their own food supply with the livestock.

In the cities, tech companies have sprung up in droves, making IT firms India's largest private-sector employer. The auto industry, software, and IT make up a significant part of the country's economy, with agriculture as the largest employer. India's economy is the fastest growing major economy in the world, thanks to an educated population, diverse resources, and the country's position within multiple facets of the digital/communications market. Customer service and helplines are one of the country's biggest exports, and it's all based on human resources. The ability of most Indians—even decades after the British Raj—to speak and write in English has had an undeniably positive effect on this particular part of India's modern economy.

Though Hindi is formally the first language of India, English and its alphabet are an almost inextricable part of the country's job market, advertising, and even the entertainment industry. The persistence of English has been good for India's growth, but its use is frustrating to many modern Indians who know full well it comes from an era of unfair colonialism. Efforts are being made by some to bolster the use of India's more historical languages, including Bengali, Konkani, and Marathi.

The caste system is still very much an ingrained part of life for the country's more than 1.3 billion residents. Concerted efforts have been made by the government, activist groups, and even religious sects, but the trenches dug by thousands of years of tradition are deep. In many cases, employers overlook the Brahmin candidates in an attempt to make up for the injustices of the past, and this only creates the opposite disparity. Still, on average, that Brahmin five percent of the population is more educated and better paid than the rest. Women are making a determined appearance in the workplace, however, and this is perhaps the positive message some employers and traditionalist families need to see to understand the benefits of letting go of some parts of the past.

The Republic of India maintains close ties with the United Kingdom but strives to develop itself once more as a land of unique resources and culture. Most citizens consider the ongoing relationship between India and the United Kingdom as positive. Many university students leave India to undertake their post-secondary studies in the UK, while Indian producers still sell spices and food items to the British who can't seem to get enough curry. The two nations interchange tourists, long-term immigrants, chefs, entrepreneurs, and much more, and that happy trade arrangement is only growing.

As for China's stolen delicacy, India remains the world's second-largest tea producer (behind China), growing 1.3 million metric tons of tea annually—that's about 1.4 million tons. What's more, they drink about 70 percent of that yield themselves, mostly as a chai mixture. Markedly different from Chinese or English tea preparations, Indian chai tea uses a blend of varied tea leaf species, brewed together with spices like cinnamon, cardamom, and cloves. When the tea is strong enough, it is sweetened delicately and finished off with a few careful drops of milk.

That fragrant, complex, and satisfying cup of chai tea is, perhaps, the perfect metaphor for a land that can take a thousand gods, billions of lifetimes, and a dozen languages and produce some of the world's most colorful, beautiful, and enduring pieces of art, literature, and history.

Free Bonus from Captivating History (Available for a Limited time)

Hi History Lovers!

Now you have a chance to join our exclusive history list so you can get your first history ebook for free as well as discounts and a potential to get more history books for free! Simply visit the link below to join.

Captivatinghistory.com/ebook

Also, make sure to follow us on Facebook, Twitter and Youtube by searching for Captivating History.

Here is another book by Captivating History that we think you would find interesting

References

"Indus-Sarasvati Civilization." The Human Journey. Retrieved from https://www.humanjourney.us/ideas-that-shaped-our-modern-world-section/early-civilizations-harappa/

"A Translation of the Edicts of Asoka." http://www.katinkahesselink.net/tibet/asoka1.html

English translation of the Brahma Net Sutra. http://www.purifymind.com/BrahmaNetSutra.htm

BBC News. "Cooking the world's oldest curry." https://www.bbc.com/news/world-asia-india-36415079

Visser, Margaret. *The Independent.* "The Ritual of Dinner: How Food can Divide Us." https://www.independent.co.uk/life-style/food-and-drink/rituals-dinner-food-eating-india-social-barriers-division-a7982406.html

The New York Times. "The Famine in India." https://www.nytimes.com/1861/03/30/archives/the-famine-in-india.html

UPI. "Natives beaten down by police in India salt bed raid." 21 May 1930. Retrieved from https://www.upi.com/Archives/1930/05/21/Natives-beaten-down-by-police-in-India-salt-bed-raid/5882104113261/.

Made in the USA
Middletown, DE
06 October 2023